Reader's Digest Paperbacks

Informative.....Entertaining.....Essential.....

Berkley, one of America's leading paperback publishers, is proud to present this special series of the best-loved articles, stories and features from America's most trusted magazine. Each is a one-volume library on a popular and important subject. And each is selected, edited and endorsed by the Editors of Reader's Digest themselves!

LAUGHTER, THE BEST MEDICINE®

THE EDITORS OF
READER'S DIGEST

BERKLEY BOOKS, NEW YORK

LAUGHTER, the Best Medicine ®
A Berkley/Reader's Digest Book, published by arrangement with
Reader's Digest Press

PRINTING HISTORY
Berkley/Reader's Digest edition / November 1981
Fifth printing / November 1982

ISBN: 0-425-05155-2

A BERKLEY BOOK ® TM 757,375
The name "BERKLEY" and the stylized "B" with design
are trademarks belonging to Berkley Publishing Corporation.
PRINTED IN THE UNITED STATES OF AMERICA

Grateful acknowledgment is made to the following organizations and individuals for permission to reprint material from the indicated sources:

Marie Rodell-Frances Collin Literary Agency for "Wedlock, Deadlock" by Jane Goodsell, copyright © 1962 by Jane Goodsell. "The Pro-Football Murder Mystery" from the book GETTING HIGH IN GOVERNMENT CIRCLES by Art Buchwald, reprinted by permission of G.P. Putnam's Sons. Copyright © 1968, 70, 71 by Art Buchwald. Mr. William Lederer for "The Best April Fool's Joke I Ever Pulled" from the book ENSIGN O'TOOLE AND ME by William Lederer, W.W. Norton Co. publishers. Copyright © 1957 by William J. Lederer. "Husband in Charge" from AT WIT'S END by Erma Bombeck. Copyright © 1974 Field Enterprises, Inc. Courtesy of Field Newspaper Syndicate. Harold Ober Associates for the following: "Oh Say, Can You Ski," copyright © 1957 by Corey Ford; "The Devious Art of Place Dropping" Copyright © 1961 by Corey Ford. Originally published as "They've Got the Drop on Me," *This Week* magazine, September, 1957. Mr. Parke Cummings for "Strong Medicine for Careless Guests" by Parke Cummings. Copyright © 1954 *This Week* magazine. Little, Brown & Company and Curtis Brown Co. for the following poems by Ogden Nash: "Yes and No", "Celery", "The Lama", "Piano Tuner, Untune Me That Tune" from the book VERSES FROM 1929 ON by Ogden Nash. Copyright © 1936 by The Curtis Publishing Co. First appeared in the *Saturday Evening Post* Copyright © 1941 By The Curtis Publishing Co. First appeared in the *Saturday Evening Post*. Copyright © 1931 by Ogden Nash. First appeared in *The New Yorker*. Copyright © by The Curtis Publishing Co. First appeared in the *Saturday Evening Post*. "The Parsnip" copyright © 1941 by The Curtis Publishing Co. First appeared in the *Saturday Evening Post*. "Inter-Office Memorandum" copyright © 1935 by Ogden Nash. First appeared in the *New York Journal-American*. "The Perfect Husband" copyright © 1949 by Ogden Nash; "Don't Cry, Darling, It's Blood All Right" copyright © 1934 by The Curtis Publishing Co. "The Kitten" copyright © 1940 by The Curtis Pub. Co.; "Everybody Makes Poets" copyright © 1935 by The Curtis Pub. Co. First appeared in the *Saturday Evening Post*. "This is Going to Hurt Just a Little Bit" from the book THE

Contents

●||●||●||●||●||●||●||●||●||●||●||●||●||●||●||●||●||●||●||●||●||●||●||●||●||●||●

●||●||●||●||●||●||●||●||●||●||●||●||●||●||●||●||●||●||●||●||●||●||●||●||●||●||●

Life in These
United States® I

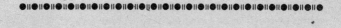

OUR newest employe, who had emigrated to this country less than three months before, told us about his first breakfast in New York:

"I sat at the counter in a midtown coffee shop, next to two gentlemen reading their newspapers. After wiping the counter, the waitress brought cups and poured coffee for each one of us. Then, without a word yet exchanged, she stood in front of the first man. 'Danish,' he said. The second man, without even raising his eyes from his paper said, 'English.' She was now standing in front of me. In a nervous voice, I whispered, 'Egyptian.'"

—Henry Sarkis *(Elmhurst, N.Y.)*

WHILE out for a drive one summer Sunday afternoon, we saw the usual number of roadside stands advertising local fruits and vegetables. Since sweet corn was just coming into season, there was a variety of signs: JUST-PICKED CORN, FRESH CORN, etc. The one that caught our eye, and our pocketbook, read: CORN—SO FRESH THE EARS STILL WIGGLE!

—Barbara A. Stalcup *(Plainsboro, N.J.)*

MOST of us Connecticut-to-New York City commuters feel that our railroad timetable is a mild form of fiction published by the management for the amusement of the regular riders. Recently, however, one early-morning train did make it to New York on time. Whereupon the man seated in front of me turned to his seatmate and said, "The train's right on schedule this morning."

"Thank goodness!" replied the other man, looking up from his newspaper. "I thought my watch had stopped."

—George Schnake *(Westport, Conn.)*

A RETIRED schoolteacher came to my uncle's used-car lot one day and looked at several different models. Instead of test-driving a car she was interested in, she would simply ask for the key, put it in the ignition, turn on the radio, start pressing the station-selector buttons. Noticing my uncle's puzzled expression, she explained: "I don't know much about cars, but their radios tell me a lot. If the stations play rock or Western music, I assume that the car has been driven hard. I buy only cars with radios set on classical or easy-listening stations—and in 17 years I've never got a lemon!"

—James Doorley *(Iowa City, Iowa)*

OUR crowd has become fascinated with all facets of astrology, and we talk a lot about it. However, one fellow didn't seem particularly impressed with our reading of horoscopes. One day, I confronted him with: "Don't you believe in astrology?"

"I think," he replied wryly, "it's a lot of Taurus."

—Mark Zimmerman *(Kingston, Pa.)*

PRIOR to the last election, my husband and I had numerous arguments about the various propositions on the California ballot. One evening, during one of these arguments, he was called to the phone. I came into the room in time to hear him say, "No, I'm not busy. Helen and I were just in the bedroom arguing over a proposition."

We have yet to live it down.

—Mrs. Emery Field *(Oroville, Calif.)*

THE following series of inter-office memos appeared on my desk on successive days:

George, Don't call—I'll be out. Forget that message I meant to give you—a change is still likely, I guess. Bill.

George, Didn't get to see you again. We pulled it all together—it'll be ready at noon. Please call me. Bill.

George, It's ready for your okay. Call me and I'll bring it over. Bill.

George, I went ahead and signed your name to the release. If Ed calls, will you see him and let me know if the package is okay? Thanks. Bill.

George, Forget the messages—*wrong George!* Bill.
—George H. Glade *(South Burlington, Vt.)*

AFTER the birth of our third child, I was extremely happy when I quickly returned to my normal weight and figure. I had been hoping for a word of praise from my husband, until one day I found him admiring himself in our long mirror. "Not bad," he was muttering. "Who would guess that I have had three children?"

—Mrs. Y. Porter

THE CHURCH I serve has a summer ministry at a chapel on Point Judith, R.I. At our first service last summer, the chairman of the board of deacons met me at the door with the information that there were no offering plates to be found. None of the men wore hats, and he thought it undignified to pass a shoe. He had tried to borrow something suitable from a house nearby, but no one was home. When I went to the chancel to begin the service, the problem was still unsolved.

Time came for the offering, and two ushers walked down the aisle wearing broad grins and carrying shiny receptacles. The deacon had resourcefully borrowed two hubcaps from a parishioner's car.

—The Rev. W. Gordon Carter *(Wakefield, R.I.)*

WE HAD moved from Chicago to a small town in Wisconsin. At the grocery store in early May, I spotted a row of petunias, each in a small pot. "How much are these?" I asked.

"Ten cents each," replied the proprietor. "But you can't buy one unless you're under 12." Noting my puzzled expression, he explained: "When I was a child, I always wanted to buy flowers for my mother on Mother's Day, but I never had enough money to go to the florist. So, each year now, I set out a few petunias for kids who have the same problem."

—Mrs. William Euting *(Fontana, Wis.)*

AFTER reading that cigar ashes make good fertilizer for house plants, my mother asked Aunt Dorothy to save some for her, since my uncle is a cigar smoker. When our family went to visit them, the ashes were forgotten until the last minute. We were in a hurry to catch a bus, so Mother wrapped the prospective fertilizer in a tissue. As we stood waiting for the bus, someone in the family asked for a tissue. Without thinking,

Mother whipped one out of her bag. The wind caught the loose end—and away went the cigar ashes. To the astonishment of the waiting group, Mother wailed, "Oh, there go Aunt Dorothy's ashes!"

—Jeanne Ashcraft *(Olympus, Wash.)*

ON A TRIP to Japan, a friend of mine called home one Sunday morning, New York time, to let his family know he had arrived safely. After speaking with his wife, he asked to talk with his 11-year-old son.

"Johnny," he said, "even though it's still only Sunday morning in New York where you are, I'm actually talking to you from tomorrow. It's Monday here in Tokyo. What do you think of that?"

"Dad," the child replied enthusiastically, "did the Jets win today?"

—R. A. Dumon *(Franklin Lakes, N.J.)*

MY BROTHER never had the inclination to be a gardener but, after moving to an area where his neighbors talked of little else, he decided to give gardening a try. He planted a few tomato plants and patiently nurtured them through the many tramplings inflicted by his two small children and the family dog. He was ecstatic when small, green tomatoes began to form.

The tomatoes were just turning red when his wife went to a hospital to give birth to their third child. Among the flowers and gifts in her room, she found an awkwardly wrapped package from her husband. Inside was a tomato, and the card with it read: "The fruit of *my* labor."

—Bob Watson *(New Braunfels, Texas)*

THE FORMER owner of our house was moving out of state, so he was delighted when we asked him to leave behind anything that he didn't want. Besides a lawnmower and several small tables, there was one item that had us bewildered. It was a board, three feet square, with two legs on one end, none on the other. I was about to toss it out, when I spotted a note taped underneath: "When you want to paint in the stairwell, this fits on the fourth step to make a level platform. Then you go across the street and borrow Schmidt's ladder."

—Don Little *(Evanston, Ill.)*

WE WERE whizzing along the New York Thruway, about an hour out of the city in pre-Fourth of July traffic, when we were passed by a bright-yellow cab. The driver sported a Hawaiian shirt, sunglasses and a big cigar. He was talking animatedly to the attractive woman beside him. The cab was full of children, suitcases and assorted vacation gear, and two bikes were strapped across the bulging trunk. Topping the mid-morning scene was the cab's brightly lighted roof sign happily proclaiming: OFF DUTY.

—Pat Street *(New York, N.Y.)*

OUR LOCAL chapter of the Sweet Adelines women's barbershop chorus was to sing at a large shopping mall. Dressed in bright-red slacks and blue-and-white middy blouses, we filed onto an escalator to ride to the lower-mall level, where a stage had been set up for our appearance. As we proceeded downward, a man standing nearby remarked to his companion, "Wow! That must have been some sale."

Barbara Waters *(Wakefield, R.I.)*

AFTER returning from a trip to Texas, a friend told about one view of the Lone Star state that he says he'll never forget. Just south of Lubbock, on the way to Houston, he passed a great field knee-high in richly green clover. Grazing in the clover was the finest herd of white-faced Hereford cattle he had ever seen. And all alone in the center of the field stood the magnificent herd bull—scratching his neck on an oil derrick.

—Jack Webb *(La Habra, Calif.)*

KNOWING that my Jewish co-worker, Morris, had married a Christian girl, I wondered how they would celebrate Christmas. As I approached their house, I could see reflections of a brightly lighted tree and I knew that Morris's new wife had had her way. But Morris had the last word: the tree was topped by a brilliant Star of David.

—Francis Hangarter *(Elizabeth, N.J.)*

Me Go Now

By BILL CONKLIN

IN THE advertising agency where I work as a copywriter, the word has long since gone around that I am vaguely daffy. It's true. I rarely say what I mean. I'm a lad who becomes involved in impossible situations. I quite literally get into things. (For example, a lamp shade once got stuck on my head in the middle of a rather exciting meeting.) And things have worsened steadily since Glenn Gordon came in as creative head of our agency.

The first time Glenn ever saw me was the day Gregory Peck toured our offices, gathering background for a movie role. At the moment I was in the art department, waiting for an artist friend to return from lunch. Sitting at a drawing board, idly drawing rectangles, I suddenly looked up to see Glenn Gordon, Gregory Peck and other important folk filing into the room. Sizing up the situation quickly, I did what I maintain was the right thing. Glenn Gordon was there to show Mr. Peck artists. I became one. I drew rectangles furiously.

"This is what we call the bull pen." Glenn said. "Here our rough ideas are rendered into finished layouts to show clients." He smiled at the artists in the bull pen. He smiled at me. Gregory Peck smiled at me. I smiled back.

As soon as they left, I decided not to wait around for the artist any longer. I scribbled a note for him to call me, took a short cut to my office and spun a piece of copy paper into my typewriter. Shadows fell across my opaque-glass cubicle. Voices murmured. I looked up, appalled. There were Glenn Gordon, Gregory Peck, the others.

"This is a typical copywriter's office," Glenn began. "Here, basic copy is pre—" He stared at me and his mouth hung open, caught on a syllable.

I smiled at him. I smiled at Gregory Peck. The group moved on and I returned to my work, but my heart wasn't in it. The battle was joined. I knew with a dread certainty that Glenn and I would meet in the lists again.

Sure enough. A week later a secretary had her purse stolen. Presuming it taken by a transient messenger and hoping at least to recover the bag, she asked me to search the wastebasket in the men's room. I went in and began looking through the big basket. Glenn Gordon entered. It didn't occur to me that he had no idea why I was examining crumpled paper towels in the lavatory of a hundred-million-dollar advertising agency. I saw it only as a good time to explain the Peck incident.

I rose up from the basket and said, "About Gregory Peck, sir. I wasn't twins the other day. I was in the art department to see about cutting up some horses." (It didn't come out right, as usual, but I *had* been there that day to get some horse photos trimmed and mounted.) Glenn backed away slowly, nodding and smiling pacifically, and bolted out the door.

After that, things went smoothly until the day we came face to face in the production department. Glenn motioned me to a chair. Obviously he needed to know more about me and, wonderfully enough, I was more than equal to the occasion. We sat calmly together and chatted easily about a variety of things. As we talked, Glenn became visibly relieved.

I decided to quit while I was ahead. I stood up quickly and leaned toward Glenn to say good-by. A simple "So long" or "Nice talking with you" would have sufficed. But as I searched for the appropriate farewell, my mind (never very stable) gave way completely. No words came. Glenn, having no inkling that I meant to leave, unable to understand why I was suddenly towering over him silently, froze like a frightened rabbit.

My mouth began to move wordlessly. Finally I managed to speak. "Me go now," I said hoarsely, and walked away.

Soon there was another incident. The time, 4:20 P.M. of a hectic day. I had just escaped from a meeting where I had warmly shaken hands with a colleague at the agency instead of the client. I was headed for the 11th floor and the sanctuary of my own office, where I often have things in control. The elevator door opened and there, naturally, was Glenn Gordon. He smiled resolutely and said, "Hi, there, how are you?"

I stepped aboard and answered, "Hi! Just getting back from lunch?"

Convene all the authors all the articles on how to succeed in business. Ask them to select the one phrase *not* to be uttered to the boss at twenty past four in the afternoon. "Just getting back from lunch?" would score an enthusiastic victory by acclamation. That was Tuesday. Wednesday was worse. I took a late lunch and celebrated a crisp January day in Manhattan by buying my fiancée a huge stuffed poodle. On my way back I saw a pair of earrings I thought she would like, and bought those, too.

It was midafternoon when I returned to my desk. Sitting there, my quixotic mind far from advertising, I had a clever idea. I decided to put the earrings on the dog's ears and thus give both presents an original touch. I unwrapped the big poodle and hoisted it up onto my desk. Carefully I took a floppy ear in my hand and began fastening a gold, bell-shaped earring to it.

Fate was tempted. Fate replied. As I bent earnestly to my task, Glenn Gordon came down the aisle and glanced in my office. Everywhere about me dedicated copywriters were hard at work. Typewriters were singing the praises of myriad products—*I* was putting earrings on a stuffed poodle. I realize now it must have been, on top of everything else, almost a traumatic experience for Glenn. I grinned a foolish grin and said noncommittally, "Dog."

In movies and plays I have often seen and admired a well-executed double take. Glenn performed not one, not two, but three takes. He stared, opened his mouth to speak, then rushed away. I have not seen him since.

CLASSIFIED CLASSICS

HEALTH-CLUB AD in the Los Angeles *Herald-Examiner:* "How's your hind site?"

FROM THE McMurray, Pa., *Advertiser:* "Flunked flute, can't toot. Took guitar, below par. Wanted: used spinet, rhythm in it."

FROM THE Saginaw, Mich., *News:* "For Sale—Eight puppies from a German Shepherd and an Alaskan Hussy."

FOR-SALE ad in the Roanoke, Ill., *Review:* "Hope chest—brand-new, half price, long story."

HELP-WANTED ad in a Michigan paper: "Adult or mature teen-ager to baby-sit. One dollar an hour—plus fridge benefits."

FROM THE Hayward, Calif., *Review:* "Found, false teeth, in parking lot at Daily Review. Please come in and smile at the switchboard operator, and she will return them to you."

FROM *The Scotchman News:* "For sale: Unicycle—still wild and untamed; mounted but never ridden."

NOTICE in the Los Altos, Calif., *Town Crier:* "Lost: Gray and white female cat. Answers to electric can opener."

PUBLIC notice in the New York *Times:* "My wife, Frances, having shared my bed and board for 20 years, is invited une-quivocally to share them for another 20."

Wedlock Deadlock

●Ⅱ●

By JANE GOODSELL

●Ⅱ●

IS MY marriage a success? Are my husband and I compatible? Did I marry the right man? Am I a good wife?

No.

My marriage doesn't even qualify as a failure. It's a disaster. But I didn't know it until I became addicted to those "Are You Happily Married?" quizzes.

Now, after 19 years of marriage and three children, it's clear that my husband and I are as mismatched a couple as the Owl and the Pussycat. If I'm honest, I can't answer a single one of the quiz questions right. I can't even answer them if I'm *dis*honest.

Question: Do you have a basic understanding about family finances?

Answer: Well, we both deplore extravagance. He deplores mine, and I deplore his.

Q: Do you share mutual interests?

A: No. His passion in life is fishing. I hate wading in that cold, wet water. He likes movies about airplanes, and I like movies about rich people. We both like to play golf, but not with each other. His jazz records give me a headache.

Q: Do you take offense easily?

A: What's "easily"? Like when I ask him if he thinks I'm too old to wear pedal pushers, and he says yes?

Q: Do you frequently nag him?

A: How else can I get him to trim the hedge?

Q: Do you have a common goal in life?

A: We would both like to be very, very rich. But we'll never make it, because we married each other.

Q: Does he do things that get on your nerves?

A: I'll say he does! He steams up the bathroom mirror when he takes a shower. He plays the stereo so loud he can't even hear me scream at him to turn it down. He leaves apple cores in ash trays.

Q: Do little things irritate him?

A: The littlest things you ever heard of. Dripping stockings hanging in the bathroom. Lost car keys. A telephone receiver left off the hook. An overdrawn checking account. Things like that.

Q: Do you feel that your role as a mother and homemaker is beneath you?

A: No. I feel it's beyond me.

Q: Do you encourage your husband in his work or profession?

A: I do my best. I keep telling him he ought to ask for a raise.

Q: Do you enjoy talking to each other?

A: Oh, we enjoy *talking* to each other all right. The problem is *listening* to each other.

Q: Do you take pains to make yourself as attractive for him as you do for a party?

A: Oh, come now—let's not be ridiculous.

Q: Do you bolster each other's confidence?

A: I keep telling him that anybody with his brains and ability can learn to fix his own breakfast. He tells me that anybody—even a mechanical moron like me—can change a fuse.

Q: When things go wrong, do you blame each other?

A: Not always. Sometimes we blame the children. Sometimes we blame Congress. Sometimes we just slam doors.

Q: Have you, through mutual patience and understanding over the years, achieved a satisfactory sexual adjustment?

A: Golly, is it *that* difficult?

"There's No Mayonnaise in Ireland"

●□●

By WILL STANTON

●□●

IF I HAVE a reputation around town for being slightly eccentric, it's because I suffer from a strange malady. In many conversations, through a kind of slip-of-the-ear, I hear things that have never been said. It usually happens when I'm talking to women, and I think it's because I'm no good at male-female banter and am constantly groping for something witty to say. As a result, I often fail to catch what is said to me. This happens especially at parties, where conversation is likely to be disjointed anyhow.

I was standing next to a woman at one party recently, not paying much attention to what she was saying, when suddenly she came out with the statement that there was no mayonnaise in Ireland.

Of course, I knew what she was doing. She had noticed that my attention was wandering, so she made up a silly remark to see if I'd let it pass. But that was a game that two could play. Without batting an eye, I came back with a strange remark of my own.

The lady made some excuse and left. Shortly afterward, I overheard her suggest to my wife that maybe I ought to be taken home. "I'm afraid he's had one too many," she said; "I was quoting a line of poetry—you know, that bit about 'No man is an island.' Well, your husband gave me a blank look and said there is no ketchup in Australia."

Then there was the time my wife sent me next door to borrow a couple of eggs, and I came back with an Easter chick.

She looked at it, and then at me. "This one's a real challenge," she said. "Let's see—you walked in without knocking...."

"Eloise was on the floor," I said, leading her on, "reaching under the bookcase...."

"That's enough," she said. "Naturally, you asked what she was doing, and she said..." My wife studied the chick. "Got it! Eloise said she was trying to catch a chick, and you said how much, and she said, 'Fifty cents,' and you said you'd cash it. So Eloise got up, you handed her 50 cents, and she said, 'Well, well, you have just bought yourself...'"

"Isn't there anything to drink in this house?" I asked.

Even when I recognize the pitfalls in time, I still have a problem. I'm thinking of the woman who told me she didn't know what to do about her husband's coffin. I didn't know what to do—or say—either. I'd have felt like a fool if I'd asked about the services and then found out that all he had was a bad cold. On the other hand, if she really *was* a widow, I didn't want to recommend some brand of cough drops. Compromising, I mumbled, "No man is an island."

"Oh?" she said. "What *do* they put on their sandwiches?"

British women are especially confusing to me. I met one at a party who mentioned that she and her husband had recently bought a neighboring farm with a very old home on it. I knew the place and asked if they were enjoying it.

"Yes," she said, "it suits us very well. We have ghosts, you know."

"No," I said, "I didn't. It's funny I've never heard about them before."

"Well," she said, "they weren't there before."

"You mean you brought them with you?"

"Yes, of course," she said. Her raised eyebrow seemed to mean that she was extra interested in our conversation, so I kept talking.

"We had one in the house when I was a boy," I said.

"You don't say," she replied. "In the house?"

"My parents always said I was imagining things, but I could hear it in the attic. Sometimes it would even come into my room."

"And it didn't bother you?"

"Oh, no," I said. "I've always been quite fond of them."

"How extraordinary!" she said.

"What's that?" It was her husband, who had just come up.

"This gentleman and I have been having a most unusual conversation," she said. "About goats."

Why, *why* can't people learn to speak clearly?

It was toward the end of the evening that I noticed an attractive girl, wearing an extremely mini outfit, sitting back in the shadows all by herself. I went over and told her how much I liked her dress.

"Thank you," she said. "I always say, you can't beat sex."

Well, I don't have to have the roof fall on me. I sat down on the couch and put my arm around her. "You took the words right out of my mouth," I said.

She seemed surprised. "Really?" she said.

"That's right," I leered. "I admire somebody who doesn't beat around the bush!" I leaned over and started to nibble her ear. The next thing I knew I got a clout on the head, and by the time I'd found my glasses the girl was gone.

Later, I heard her talking to the hostess. "I don't know what set him off," she was saying. "I said that I'd bought my dress at Saks, and—wow!—it was Katie bar the door!"

So now I've become overly cautious. If a woman says, "I'm *so* proud of my knees," I pause; I think; and then I remember with a smile that she happens to have a nephew, too.

On occasion, however, I'm still baffled. Like the time last summer when my wife and children were at the shore and I was alone in the house. The phone rang, and a sultry voice said, "This is Sophia Loren. I just got into town, and I'd like to stop by and see you."

Actually, I don't know what the voice said, because obviously it couldn't have been what it sounded like. So I said I was sorry, I was sick, and I hung up.

Since then I have gone over that message word by word, trying to see what part of it I could have misunderstood. As far as I can tell, it means exactly what it seems to have meant. I read in the paper that Sophia *was* in town that evening, and it certainly did sound like her voice.

Of course, I know perfectly well that if I'd said, "Okay, sure," it would have turned out that I'd ordered aluminum siding for the house and garage. Or agreed to take charge of PTA entertainment for the next year. Something like that.

At least, that's what I keep telling myself.

The Pro-Football
Murder Mystery

●II●II●II●II●II●II●II●II●II●II●II●II●II●II●II●II●II●II●II●II●II●II●II●

By ART BUCHWALD

●II●II●II●II●II●II●II●II●II●II●II●II●II●II●II●II●II●II●II●II●II●II●II●

As DETECTIVE Peter Minderman stared at the color-television set in the simple living room of the Socalaw house, he was baffled. The body of Artie Socalaw was still in the same chair where he had died. All the suspects in the case were there: Artie's wife, Emma, and Artie's best friends, George Stevens, Jr., Chuck McDermott, Sam Markay and Tony Valenti.

"All right," said detective Minderman. "Let's start from the beginning. You guys began watching pro football two days ago on Saturday noon, right in this living room."

"That's correct," said Stevens. "Then, suddenly, Sunday night, somewhere during the third quarter of the Raider game, we noticed there was something wrong with Artie. We waited until the game ended at seven, and then went over to his chair. He was dead."

"It was a shock, coming after the 49ers' defeat of the Vikings," Chuck McDermott added.

"But," said detective Minderman, "the coroner said Artie had been dead for 24 hours. How come no one discovered it before then?"

"Artie was always quiet when he watched a pro-football game," said Sam Markay. "He wasn't one to holler and shout after each play. So, when he didn't say anything for 24 hours, we figured he was just suffering because Dallas beat the Lions."

"When you're watching pro football on TV," said Tony Valenti, "you don't notice whether people are breathing or not."

15

Detective Minderman looked over at Mrs. Socalaw. "When did you last see your husband alive?"

"You mean moving around and that sort of thing?" Mrs. Socalaw asked. "It was in July, before the exhibition games started. He hasn't left that chair since the Redskins played the Patriots in a pre-season game. I don't wish to dispute the coroner's report, but I thought Artie was dead three months ago."

"Just before the Baltimore-Cincinnati game," Stevens said, "Artie asked me if I wanted a piece of fruitcake."

"Where did the fruitcake he had come from?" asked Minderman.

"I made it," said Mrs. Socalaw. "I always make fruitcake during the holiday season. It helps me forget."

"Did anyone else eat any?"

"I did," said McDermott.

"No ill effects?"

"None that I can tell," McDermott said.

"Damn!" said Minderman. "There goes the poisoned-fruitcake theory. Did he eat anything else?"

"I gave him a tuna-fish sandwich," McDermott said.

"A what?"

"A tuna-fish sandwich. Mrs. Socalaw refuses to feed us, so we bring our own food. This time my wife made me a tuna-fish sandwich," McDermott said.

"Don't you know what's going on with tuna fish?" Minderman asked.

"I'm not much for fishing. The only sport I watch is football," McDermott said.

"Your wife tried to knock you off with a mercury-poisoned tuna-fish sandwich," detective Minderman said. "But Artie became the victim, instead of you."

"I knew she was sore at me," McDermott said, "but I didn't think she'd go that far."

Minderman went to the phone and called the McDermott house. "Mrs. McDermott, I'm sending someone over to arrest you for the tuna-fish murder of Artie Socalaw."

Mrs. Socalaw grabbed the phone. "Don't worry, Gloria!" she shouted. "I'll testify in your behalf. We can always say it was a crime of passion."

SUPERDUPER BLOOPERS

ON A NEWSCAST a Kentucky announcer stated: "The Stork Club, located on Seventh Street here in Louisville, has had its leer and bicker license revoked...."

—Contributed by Mrs. Rex Layne

AN ANNOUNCER on a Gainesville, Fla., radio station delighted his audience with the following launderette commercial: "Ladies who care to drive by and drop off their clothes will receive prompt and individual attention."

—Contributed by Mrs. H. B. Black

SHERIFF addressing a TV audience in a Florida town: "I will wipe out prostitution if I have to tie up all my men to do it."

A JACKSON, Miss., TV announcer, advertising a local bank: "Save a part of every pay check. Save *now* for the better things in life—a home, a trip, a broad, or a new car."

A CONTESTANT on a quiz show in St. Paul mentioned that the population of her home town had remained the same for a number of years. "Every time a baby is born, someone leaves town," she explained.

—Contributed by William B. Keonen, Jr.

Rolling in the Isles

MIROSLAV BARTÁK
GREAT CARTOONS OF THE WORLD (CROWN)

"He won't leave without Sandra!"
SAXON, REGISTER AND TRIBUNE SYNDICATE

"That's the best damned forced landing I've ever seen!"
SCHOGRET, B. P. SINGER FEATURES

A Little Surprise
for the Girls

●II●II●II●II●II●II●II●II●II●II●II●II●II●II●II●II●II●II●II●II●II●II●II●

By THOMAS BOLTON

●II●II●II●II●II●II●II●II●II●II●II●II●II●II●II●II●II●II●II●II●II●II●II●

WE TOOK our seats in the breakfast nook with all the spontaneous gaiety of delegates arriving at the Strategic Arms Limitation Talks. Surrounded by females, I awaited the opening gun in the discussion of Item 1 on the agenda: Cathy's upcoming birthday and the entertainment relating thereto.

Cathy, almost nine, a bulldog spirit in the body of a princess, cleared her throat. "At Andrea's birthday party," she announced, "they had a magician."

"Tricks, Daddy!" cried five-year-old Betsy, eyes popping out of her sweet face.

"Tricks," I echoed. "Watch the expensive magician make Daddy's money disappear. Now listen, all of you. This household is not funded by the Ford Foundation. We are trying to economize. That's why I am painting the basement myself and why your poor mother is making her own clothes."

Wife Liz sighed prettily in a neutral corner, holding the baby, who was ominously, uncharacteristically, quiet.

"At Patty's party," Cathy intoned methodically, "they had a clown. They even had a *monkey*."

"Monkeys don't grow on trees," I shot back. Liz opened her mouth to say something, then closed it.

"At Beverly's party," Cathy continued, "we all had neat rides..."

"Enough!" I said calmly. "Birthday parties in this family are *not* going to be Broadway extravaganzas. A simple cake,

flights in Vancouver to verify passengers' documents.

KIM BOLAN
Vancouver Sun

The federal government crackdown on airlines bringing people to Canada without proper documents could prevent legitimate refugees from finding safe haven here, the president of the Vancouver Refugee Council said Monday.

"The air carrier sanctions are designed to keep legitimate refugees out," said Phil Rankin, an immigration lawyer. "This violates the spirit of the whole convention on refugees."

Immigration officials confirmed last week that they are boarding international flights at Vancouver International Airport and elsewhere at least once a day to check the documents of passengers.

If someone is found without legitimate papers, they can still make a refugee claim in Canada. But the airline is fined up to $3,200 a person and must pay the costs of sending the per-

JUST THE FACTS

Claire Winstone's funny bone got tickled recently.
She sent along some "facts of life" to share with our
readers:

- ☐ If you are given an open-book exam, you will forget your book.
- ☐ Always remember to pillage BEFORE you burn.
- ☐ The two most common elements in the universe are hydrogen and stupidity.
- ☐ If at first you don't succeed, skydiving is not for you.
- ☐ Psychiatrists say that one of four people is mentally ill. Check three friends. If they're okay, you're it.
- ☐ Nothing in the known universe travels faster than a bad cheque.
- ☐ A truly wise man never plays leapfrog with a unicorn.
- ☐ The trouble with doing something right the first time is that nobody appreciates how difficult it was.
- ☐ The average woman would rather have beauty than brains, because the average man can see better than he can think.
- ☐ Clothes make the man. Naked people have little or no influence on society.

a few good friends, singing, a party game or two. What's wrong with Pin the Tail on the Donkey?"

"Oh, Daddy!" Cathy writhed with embarrassment. "That's prehis—toric!"

"It built this nation's character, young lady, and don't you forget it. We are going to keep things simple around here, and that's final. Are there any questions?"

"Yes," said Betsy thoughtfully. "Is the tooth fairy a girl or a boy?"

As I groped for a reply, the baby suddenly shot her hand into her mother's egg cup and extracted a wet fistful. Liz's shriek rattled the crockery, and Betsy spilled her 62nd consecutive glass of milk. I lit out for the peace and quiet of rush-hour traffic.

I didn't think again about the birthday festivities until I was kissing Liz good-night. "Sweet dreams, J. P. Morgan," she said.

When you've been married a few years, you sense veiled sarcasm. "You think I'm being too hard on Cathy?" I asked.

"I just hope she doesn't feel we're letting her down," Liz answered. "That we don't *care.*"

"Honey, I'll tell you what—I'll take personal charge of the party. I'll organize it, keep things moving so that everyone's happy." I had this sudden vision of myself, kindly and serene, surrounded by merry little girls in party dresses. "I'll show Cathy that I have a deep interest in her party—and teach her a lesson about economy in the bargain. Just leave everything to me."

Liz mumbled something into her pillow that sounded like "God save us all."

The great day dawned cold and snowy. The party was to begin at four. At noon I was lying on the sofa, made dizzy by blowing up 50 balloons and wondering about brain damage from oxygen starvation. Still, I was obviously able to think with all my old power and clarity. "We'll organize things in the basement," I explained, with a smile to show that all was under control. Cathy beamed. I had her full confidence.

At four sharp, the doorbell rang. (Adults may like to be fashionably late, but at a children's birthday party the participants are as punctual as lawyers.) First to arrive was little

Abigail, a pudgy child with a voice of wondrous resonance and power. "Is there gonna be a magician?" she asked.

"No, no. We're going to make our own fun today."

"You're a brave man," Abigail's mother said to me before she disappeared.

Then all the other children arrived at once, darting past my legs like bright-colored tropical fish to offer their presents to a joyous Cathy, who opened them in a tumult of squeals and giggles.

After 15 minutes or so, I cupped hands to mouth and shouted, "To the basement we go!" It was really quite gay down there, with clusters of Daddy's breath wrapped in bright balloons and strung along the freshly painted blue walls, and card tables set with flowers awaiting the ice cream and cake.

The little girls milled about noisily. Finally, I captured their attention and began, "First of all, girls, we're going to play Duck, Duck, Goose. The rules are relatively simple. We . . ."

Cathy was tugging at my sleeve. "I'm going to put on a record," she said. "We can play games after we dance and have the cake. I know a specially good game."

As the phonograph began a caterwauling ode to a defunct motorcycle, I went up the basement stairs. It was like ascending from the seventh ring of Dante's inferno. Liz was in the kitchen, candling the cake. "I thought you were going to stay down there to keep things moving," she said.

"High time Cathy learned to stand on her own two feet," I said as I kicked off my shoes, turned on television and settled down to watch the Giants and the Packers.

At halftime I wandered about the house, and found myself facing the hall closet, repository of the old football helmet I keep in case a son ever comes along. On impulse I reached for it and jammed it on my head. Terrifically tight around both ears—damned if I could get it off!

At that moment, Liz entered to announce, "The cake has been gobbled up. If I'm not interrupting anything important, I could use your help. I want to get this skirt hemmed. It's a wrap-around, so it will fit even you."

Before I could say anything, she had swirled a flowered skirt around my waist. "You look silly," she giggled through a mouthful of pins.

Suddenly, from deep in the bowels of the house, there arose a piercing scream that would have sent chills through Alfred

Hitchcock. Barefoot, I raced down the basement stairs—into well-black darkness.

"What happened?" I shouted. "Who's hurt?"

"No one, Daddy," Cathy called from over near the furnace. "We're playing Murder in the Dark. Abigail got murdered."

I stepped along the wall toward the light switch. Sudden wetness engulfed my left foot. A flash of intuition told me that it was paint. Blue paint. Damn near a full bucket. Before my hand could reach the switch, the lights blazed on. At the head of the stairs stood Abigail's mother—her eyes taking in my blue foot, the flowered skirt, the helmet.

Abigail herself shrieked with delight. "Oh, neat—Cathy's daddy is playing a clown! A clown show, a clown show!"

"A little surprise for the girls," I said weakly, as Abigail's mother studied me carefully. Then, with as much horror as surprise, I found myself executing a shuffling little dance step. Helmet bobbing, skirt flouncing, blue foot splatting time, I began to sing a song that had once failed to lull Cathy to sleep: "De Camptown ladies sing dis song, Doo-dah! doo-dah! De Camptown racetrack five miles long, Oh! doo-dah-day!"

The girls shouted with laughter. Calls for more greeted my concluding curtsy. So I gave them "Waltzing Matilda"—I'm the only person I know who knows all the words. Despite pleas for an encore, I cut it short. Other mothers were appearing, studying me from the kitchen heights with much the same transfixed expression as Abigail's mother.

When all the guests had at last departed, Cathy gave me a thankful hug, and Liz helped me tug the helmet free. "A star is born," she said, with that knack she has for summing things up.

Later, Cathy and I had a long talk. "True fun isn't something you can buy," I pointed out. "How much better to make the good times happen all by themselves!" I went on like that for quite a while, and her thoughtful eyes never left mine. She seemed to hang on every word. "You learned something today, didn't you, Cathy?" I concluded gently.

"Yes, Daddy." Then, reality. "You know," she went on, "it must be the light or something, but when you hold your head that way and I hold mine this way, I see a great picture of myself in your glasses."

HOW THEY TALK!

REV. Oscar Johnson, jovial St. Louis pastor, tells this on himself:

Once, after a change of churches, he met a woman of his former flock and asked, "How do you like your new pastor?"

"Just fine," she beamed. "But somehow or other, he just doesn't seem to *hold* me like you did!"

—Contributed by John Newton Baker

AS WE DROVE along a Los Angeles thoroughfare lined with spectacular advertising signs, our nine-year-old exclaimed: "Look at all the bullboards!"

—Contributed by Mrs. Paul A. Cuilhe

A JUNIOR MISS, exposed for the first time to the musical life of the Berkshires, wrote home: "Of all the musical compositions I have heard the one I like best is 'The Damn Nation of Faust' by Berlioz."

—Contributed by Dale Warren

MY SWIMMING instructor at a Los Angeles university was quizzing a group of us on Red Cross life saving and water safety techniques. We answered all her questions easily until she posed this one: "Which article of clothing would you remove last if you were catapulted from a boat or dock fully clothed?"

Everyone mentioned something different. It was evident that we didn't know, so the instructor helped us. "The blouse," she said, "because the air gets under the blouse and acts like a buoy!"

The subsequent uproar ended the class.

—Contributed by Doris Wightman

Laughter, the Best Medicine® I

AT A trial in Detroit's Recorder's Court, a young woman who had accused the defendant of making an improper proposal was asked to state the question that allegedly had been asked. It embarrassed her to repeat it, so she was permitted to write it on a piece of paper. After the judge, prosecutor and defense counsel had read it, it was passed to the jury. Each juror read it, and gave it to the next juror.

After an attractive female juror had read it, she attempted to pass it to the man on her right, but found him dozing. Without comment, she nudged him and gave him the slip of paper. The awakened juror read the note, smiled at her, nodded, and put the note in his pocket!

—Contributed by Richard E. Schaft

A YOUNG physician's custom was to drop into a bar after office hours and order a daiquiri cocktail with nutmeg sprinkled over it. One evening the bartender discovered that he was out of nutmeg, but he did have a bowl of mixed nuts on the back bar. He grated a hickory nut over the daiquiri and handed it to the doctor.

After a sip, the doctor said, "What's this?"

"A *hickory* daiquiri, doc," was the reply.

—Contributed by Philip C. Humphrey

THE OLD Milwaukee Brewers once had a pitcher named Mel Faimey. He was pitching brilliantly one hot, sultry August day,

25

when a fan slipped him a beer between innings. Subsequently, he had several more bottles, and his pitching became erratic. By the ninth inning, he'd completely lost control, and walked several batters to give the opposing team the victory.

On the way to the dugout, one of the players on the other team saw the case of empties, and said to his teammate, "Look, there's the beer that made Mel Faimey walk us."

—Contributed by Mitchell Smith

WHEN my granddaughter was 13, and about to attend a dance at her school, she told her parents, "Most of the girls are inviting boys, but I have decided to go a stray."

—Contributed by I. Paul Taylor

AT AN exhibit of abstract art at The Jewish Museum in New York City, I was standing before a large blob of plastic. Two Jewish matrons came up. After a moment of silence, one turned to the other and said in a distressed tone. "That's Jewish?"

—Contributed by Robert McMillan

SIGNS OF LIFE

ON THE gate of a pasture evidently used as a lovers' lane: "Please close the gate. The heifer you're chasing is easier to catch than mine!"

—Contributed by Joanne Boysen

HANDWRITTEN sign on a soft-drink vending machine: "Beware! This Machine Is Coiniverous!"

—Contributed by Louise Hankins

BY A MOTEL in Plymouth, Mass.: "Come in and take a road off your mind."

—Contributed by Jean Rockwood

The Unicorn
in the Garden

●‖●‖●‖●‖●‖●‖●‖●‖●‖●‖●‖●‖●‖●‖●‖●‖●‖●‖●‖●

By JAMES THURBER

●‖●‖●‖●‖●‖●‖●‖●‖●‖●‖●‖●‖●‖●‖●‖●‖●‖●‖●‖●

ONCE upon a sunny morning a man looked up from his scrambled eggs to see a white unicorn with a gold horn quietly cropping the roses in the garden. The man went to the bedroom where his wife was still asleep and woke her. "There's a unicorn in the garden," he said. "Eating roses." She opened one unfriendly eye and looked at him. "The unicorn is a mythical beast," she said. The man walked slowly out into the garden. The unicorn was still there. "Here, unicorn," said the man, and he pulled up a lily and gave it to him. The unicorn ate it gravely. With a high heart, because there was a unicorn in his garden, the man roused his wife again. "The unicorn," he said, "ate a lily." His wife sat up in bed and looked at him, coldly. "You are a booby," she said, "and I am going to have you put in the booby hatch." The man who had never liked the words "booby" and "booby hatch," thought for a moment. "We'll see about that," he said. He walked to the door. "He has a golden horn in the middle of his forehead," he told her. Then he went back to the garden to watch the unicorn; but the unicorn had gone away.

The wife got up and dressed as fast as she could. She was very excited and there was a gloat in her eye. She telephoned the police and she telephoned a psychiatrist; she told them to hurry to her house and bring a strait jacket. When the police and the psychiatrist arrived they sat down and looked at her, with great interest. "My husband," she said, "saw a unicorn this morning." The police looked at the psychiatrist and the psychiatrist looked at the police. "He told me it ate a lily," she said. The psychiatrist looked at the police and the police looked at the psychiatrist. "He told me it had a golden horn in the middle of its forehead," she said. At a solemn signal from the psychiatrist, the police leaped from their chairs and seized the wife. She put up a terrific struggle, but they finally got her into the strait jacket just as the husband came back.

"Did you tell your wife you saw a unicorn?" asked the police. "Of course not," said the husband. "The unicorn is a mythical beast." "That's all I wanted to know," said the psychiatrist. "Take her away. I'm sorry, sir, but your wife is as crazy as a jay bird." So they took her away, cursing and screaming, and shut her up in an institution. The husband lived happily ever after.

Moral: Don't count your boobies until they are hatched.

COLLEGE CAPERS

I BEGAN my last semester of college six months pregnant. Walking down the hall in the psychology buildilng one day, I was grabbed from behind and spun around to face a totally strange young man. His eyes fastened on my protruding midriff; his face paled; his books dropped to the floor. I shook his arm and asked if he was all right. He looked at my face, then whooped and swung me around in a bear hug. "Thank God!" he said. "You're someone else!"

—Contributed by M. C. Davenport

MY COLLEGE-AGE SON is an avid rock-music fan. So I was a bit surprised when, returning from work on the first day of his vacation from Princeton, I found him listening to a Beethoven symphony. Pretty classy university, I thought to myself, to manage such a transition in a matter of weeks. Next day, I was greeted by Beethoven again, this time the violin concerto. I couldn't resist commenting. "Wow, Mike," I said, "Princeton certainly has done wonders for your musical taste."

"Well, Dad, I didn't have too much choice," he replied morosely. "I took all the good records to college."

—Contributed by R. A. H.

Humor in Uniform I

THERE WAS a water shortage in Kodiak, and an order came from the commanding general that passes and liberty would be canceled until the water supply was back to normal. All the armed forces complied except a small outpost of Seabees, about 30 in number, under the command of a rough-and-ready chief warrant officer. Saturday evening came and the Seabees stormed the nearly abandoned city, only to be rounded up by MP's and returned to their base. The chief warrant officer was brought before the provost marshal and asked if he had received the general's order.

"Yes, sir."

"Then why didn't you comply?" roared the provost.

"Well, sir, I didn't think it applied to us."

"And why not?"

"Because my men don't drink no water when they go into town, sir," replied the chief.

—Robert L. Jamison *(Columbus, Ohio)*

A NEWLY TRAINED B-17 pilot, upon arrival in England during World War II, asked a veteran of many missions over Germany, "How good is the fighter escort for our bombers?"

"Man, you've got the best fighter escort in the world," the veteran replied. "The RAF escorts you to the English Channel. The Luftwaffe meets you there and escorts you all the way to the target and back again. Then the Americans pick you up and escort you home!"

—Richard T. Sanborn *(Short Hills, N.J.)*

MY NIECE invited me to meet the young serviceman who was courting her. "I love Sam," she said, "but somehow I'm not sure of our future together. I'd like your opinion of him."

Sam arrived and proved himself a charming young man, although extremely nervous over meeting the first of the relatives. During dinner he capsized his water glass, dropped his fork twice, spilled his coffee, then burned my nose in his eagerness to light my cigarette. Nevertheless, when he had gone, I pronounced him good solid husband material. "Even if he is the original butterfingers," I added.

"That's just what I mean about our future," said my niece. "Sam is in a bomb disposal unit!"

—K. Clem Hopkins *(Portland, Ore.)*

DURING the Allied occupation of Vienna, a streetcar was passing through the American Zone of the city. The conductor, noticing a GI among the passengers, decided to provide a little entertainment for the Austrians on board. Every time the car passed an American installation, he would call out its name with an atrocious pseudo-American accent and then give its former Austrian title. "Silver Dollar Club, formerly Café Goethe," "Yankee Sports Center, formerly the Messepalast," "Yank Cinema, formerly Kolloseum Lichtspielhaus" and so on.

The GI paid no attention to the commentary or to the broad grins of his fellow passengers, but continued to read his *Stars and Stripes*. Just before reaching his stop, however, he stood up, turned to the occupants and in very passable German said politely, "Auf Wiedersehen, formerly Heil Hitler!"

—L. H. Adams *(Vienna, Austria)*

AT THE height of World War II, some British MP's protested indignantly in the House of Commons because Field Marshal Bernard L. Montgomery had entertained a defeated Italian general at dinner. After listening for a time, Winston Churchill, who is known for his love of a good table while Montgomery is something of an ascetic, rose and addressed the House: "I do not know if the honorable member who is complaining has ever had dinner with Montgomery. I have, and my sympathies are entirely with the Italian general!"

—Geoffrey Daukes *(Sevenoaks, Kent, England)*

AT AN Army survival lecture, the instructor was saying, "Grasshoppers are not only edible but highly nutritious. In fact, King Solomon used to feed them to all his wives. Grasshoppers made them healthy and alert."

A voice from the rear interrupted: "To hell with what they fed the wives—what did they feed King Solomon?"

—Henry E. Leabo *(Represa, Calif.)*

DURING basic training for the Army Nurse Corps, we were required to spend one week in the field roughing it. It rained the entire week. We arose daily in our swampy tent, took a cold-water beauty bath from our helmets, donned our pistol belts and ponchos, and trudged through the mud to set up field hospitals. Obviously, our personal appearance frequently left much to be desired.

The final blow to our feminine pride occurred while we waited in the mess line in the mud and rain. A young private came by with a camera and asked to take our picture. "It will prove to my girl," he said, "that she has *no* reason to be jealous!"

—Catherine G. Lutes *(Tallmadge, Ohio)*

A SAILOR who limped into the Naval dispensary had his foot X-rayed and was asked to wait for the results. A while later a corpsman appeared and handed the sailor a large pill. Just then a mother with a child in need of immediate attention entered. After the corpsman disappeared with the new patient, the sailor hobbled over to the drinking fountain, swallowed the pill and sat down to wait. Some time later the corpsman reappeared, carrying a bucket of water. "Okay," he said. "Let's drop the pill in this bucket and soak that foot."

—Mrs. H. E. Hicks *(Inglewood, Calif.)*

WE WERE sitting around at the NCO club discussing security procedures and what type of security clearances we held.

One sergeant said, "I'm cleared for rumors up to and including ridiculous."

—Sgt. W. P. Hess, USAF *(APO, San Francisco, Calif.)*

AT HAMPTON ROADS, where I was attached to a small minesweeper that regularly passed by old Fort Monroe while sweeping Thimble Shoals Channel, the discussion turned to the difference between a "fort" and a "fortress." An old Army sergeant aboard for combined Army-Navy exercises had the question put to him.

"It's perfectly simple," he replied. "If it has breastworks, it's a fortress."

—Capt. Harvey Headland, USN *(Bellevue, Wash.)*

IT WAS the first day at an Army basic-training site, and a coarse-voiced first sergeant was giving the troops an indoctrination toward adjusting to Army life. "First thing I want to say," he growled, "is that there will be no, I repeat, *no,* demonstrations or indications of bias, bigotry or prejudice in this man's Army. Every man here is equal, and any man who acts different will be severely disciplined—especially you nuts from California."

—Roland C. Rustch *(Arabi, La.)*

DID YOU HEAR...

... about the billing clerk who went to a psychiatrist—he kept hearing strange invoices.

—Robert Orben

... about the sequel to *The Godfather*—it's called "War and Pizza."

—Shelby Friedman

How Did I Get to Be 40?

By JUDITH VIORST

No More Babies

The sterilizer's up for grabs.
Nicked portacrib, good-bye.
My third and youngest son is growing older.
I'm done with dawn awakenings,
With pablum in my eye,
With small moist bundles burping on my shoulder.

I gave away my drawstring slacks
And smocks with floppy bows.
My silhouette will never more be pear-ish.
And though I'm left with stretch marks
And a few veins varicose,
I'm aiming for an image less ma-mère-ish.

No playpens in the living room
Will mangle my décor.
My stairs will not be blocked with safety fences.
No rattles, bottles, bibs, stuffed bears
Will disarray my floor,
No eau de diaper pail assail my senses.

33

And no more babies will disrupt
The tenor of my day,
Nor croup and teething interrupt my sleeping.
I swear to you I wouldn't have it
Any other way.
It's positively stupid to be weeping.

Among Other Thoughts
on Our Wedding Anniversary

Over the years,
When the sink overflowed
Or the car ran out of gas
Or the lady who comes every Tuesday to clean didn't come
Or I felt pudgy
Or misunderstood
Or inferior to Marilyn Kaufman who is not only a pediatric
    surgeon but also a very fine person as well as beautiful
Or I fell in the creek and got soaked on our first family
    camping trip
Or mosquitoes ate me alive on our first family camping trip
Or I bruised my entire left side on our first family camping
    trip
Or I walked through a patch of what later turned out to be
    plenty of poison ivy on what later turned out to be our
    last family camping trip
Or my sweater shrank in the wash
Or I stepped on my glasses
Or the keys that I swear on my children's head I put on the
    top of the dresser weren't there
Or I felt depressed
Or unfulfilled
Or inferior to Ellen Jane Garver who not only teaches consti-
    tutional law but is also a wit plus sexually insatiable
Or the rinse that was going to give my hair some subtle copper
    highlights turned it purple

Or my mother-in-law got insulted at something I said
Or my stomach got upset at something I ate
Or I backed into a truck that I swear when I looked in
   my rear-view mirror wasn't parked there
Or I suffered from some other blow of fate,
It's always been so nice to have my husband by my side so I
   could
Blame him.

Alone

Alone I could own both sides of the double bed
And stay up reading novels half the night.
And no one would be here telling me turn off the light
And hogging the blankets.

And no one would be here saying he's taking the car
And noticing that I let the milk turn sour.
Alone I could talk long distance for an hour
And who would stop me?

And no one would be here brushing his teeth with my brush
And pushing the thermostat down to sixty degrees.
Alone I could give Goodwill my boots and my skis
And switch to beaches.

Alone I could give up understanding Brie,
Détene, the Superbowl, and Cousin Rose.
And no one would be here telling me which of my clothes
Make me look chunky.

And no one would be here steaming the bathroom up
And wanting his back massaged and his buttons sewn.
And no one would be here. I would be alone.
And I would hate it.

Par for the Course

"Well, there goes civilization!"
ED FISHER IN *THE SPECTATOR*, ENGLAND

"I said, 'Only if it rains'!"
MEREDITH OATES FEATURES

"Nasty slice."
JERRY MARCUS IN *THE SATURDAY EVENING POST*

"His psychological game is pure murder."
HERB GREEN IN *THE SATURDAY EVENING POST*

"But, George, it's just a game!"
VIRGIL PARTCH, PUBLISHERS-HALL SYNDICATE

Great-Granddad's Last Battle

By ROBERT FROMAN

ONE OF THE most memorable occasions of my youth in Caldwell, Idaho, was the Saturday afternoon I took my great-grandfather to his first picture show. I was nine or ten, and "Granddad," as he was known to his several generations of descendants, was in his 90's. The show was a "Wild Western," and that afternoon the term proved gloriously apt.

Granddad had been a more or less commissioned officer in a body of irregular Confederate troops in Missouri in 1863, and he tended to hark back to those days when he got excited or when he was in a storytelling mood. My first memory of him is of a day when my mother left me with him at his cabin while she went shopping. He was impressively gaunt, with a bony, Bible-prophet face set off by sparse, shoulder-length white hair. I was scared of him at first; but, after Mother departed, he got out his corncob pipe and sack of mullein leaf, and, as I watched, he slowly stuffed the bowl, lit it, took a couple of puffs and passed it to me. From that moment I was his to command.

On the afternoon I took him to his first movie we were a bit late. The lights had already been dimmed, and the pianist, a young music student at the local college, was running through her practice chords. I guided Granddad down the aisle to the front row. By the time he was settled, the feature was opening with Hoot Gibson riding across the range. I glanced sideways for Granddad's reaction. He was completely spellbound.

The plot thickened fast when the camera switched to a stage-coach moving toward an armed ambush. As the villains prepared to pounce, the pianist quickened the rhythm. Suddenly Granddad rose to his feet and let out a piercing rebel yell to warn the stage driver.

The pianist turned to behold, looming over her, about three feet away, a tall, tottery figure with arms flung wide, a three-day growth of white beard, and a wild look in his deep-sunk eyes. With a screech the girl leaped from bench to keyboard to piano top, and thence to the stage, where she stumbled through the stretched sheet that served as the screen, tearing open a large flap.

Except for Granddad the audience of perhaps 40 included no one older than 12. The unscheduled hullabaloo suggested that we ought to do something, too. But what? The action on the wounded screen showed us. Riding in pursuit of the villains, Hoot jumped, fell or was shot from his horse right into the hole created by the pianist, and a friend of mine named Vergil climbed up to see what had become of him. Three or four others followed Vergil. They had just made it when the scene on the untorn part of the screen switched to a view of the villains riding off with their loot. Vergil pulled his cap pistol and let them have it.

Since the Fourth of July was approaching, nearly all of us were armed with cap pistols and well supplied with caps. Under ordinary circumstances we would never have thought of firing our guns inside the theater. But now, with the villains still on the screen, Granddad turned to his troops and called for a barrage.

The firing quickly brought the ticket-taker. In those days motion-picture film was highly flammable; when the ticket-taker saw the smoke from our caps, he dashed out of the theater yelling, "Fire!" When we heard his cries, we thought he was urging us on.

At last Granddad gave the command to cease firing. "No sense wasting your ammunition when they're running away!" he shouted. "Wait till they come sneaking back."

It was not long in coming. The villains reappeared on the scene, and Granddad, standing crane-tall in the front row, instructed us to prepare to fire.

At that moment half a dozen store clerks and passersby, led by the town constable, entered the theater through the back door. The piano player's hysterical description of what awaited them had inclined the members of this posse to be careful, and the darkness of the theater added to their caution. It was justified, for when the constable stuck his head through the torn screen, he was greeted by a ragged volley of cap-pistol fire.

Just then a fireman entered from the lobby, a fire-hoze nozzle cradled in his arms. In the gloom he smelled smoke. "Water!" he shouted to his mates behind, and he turned the full force of it on the screen as he and his helpers dragged the hose down the left aisle.

"Make way for the artillery!" Granddad yelled. "Maintain covering fire!"

By this time there was not enough left of the screen to give us more than an occasional glimpse of the top of someone's head or a horse's tail. But we scarcely noticed the loss, for the drenched constable and his cohorts made fine targets. We fell back up the right aisle until we had used all our ammunition, then retreated to the street and marched off with Granddad to his cabin for a lengthy reminiscing about our battle experiences.

All of us looked forward to another skirmish the next Saturday afternoon, but Granddad never again would join us at the movies. He said they were too noisy.

HOME TRUTH

You CAN'T fully comprehend the phrase "million-dollar smile" until you've had a child in orthodontic braces.

—Jean Walter

The Best April Fool's Joke
I Ever Pulled

●II●II●II●II●II●II●II●II●II●II●II●II●II●II●II●II●II●II●II●II●II●II●II●

By W. J. LEDERER

●II●II●II●II●II●II●II●II●II●II●II●II●II●II●II●II●II●II●II●II●II●II●II●

IT WAS the morning of April 1, 1939, and our destroyer, the USS *Appleby*, swung around her anchor in Manila Bay. In the wardroom a heated debate was under way. We officers had a problem to solve before the captain returned to the ship.

"We've *got* to find a way to scroggle him," said the first lieutenant. "April Fool's Day is our only chance—we may never get another legitimate shot at the old buzzard."

I should point out that we loved our commanding officer, Lt. Cmdr. J. J. Sweeney. No ship ever had a better skipper. But Sweeney had a passion for practical jokes, and, at one time or another, had successfully shafted all the officers on the *Appleby*. In my case, he had subscribed to a Lonely Hearts Association in my name. He intercepted replies and carried on a correspondence until I finally received a telegram from a widow with four children—saying she was flying from Arizona to Manila to marry me.

We all agreed that on this first of April we had to hang a deluxe, extra-special gag on the old boy. The medical officer (the captain had once put a snapping beetle in his stethoscope) suggested mixing a purgative in the captain's oatmeal. The chief engineer recommended loosening the propeller nut in the gig, so that after the captain started ashore the propeller would drop off and leave him adrift.

These, I felt, were schoolboy plots.

Here's the way I had it figured. The captain owned a home in Manila, and he delighted in having his wife and children there with him. He hated the ship's annual summer cruise to

42

China. For one thing, it isolated him from his family; for another, it subjected him to Chinese food, which he loathed.

These facts left no doubt in my mind about how to hoax the captain. We'd send him to China.

As communications officer, it was no trouble for me to fake a radio dispatch detaching Commander Sweeney from the *Appleby* and sending him to Chungking, 1600 miles into the interior of China. After breakfast, the communications messenger handed the captain the morning's radio traffic. In the pile was my message. LT COMDR J J SWEENEY USN DETACHED 9 APRIL AS COMMANDING OFFICER USS APPLEBY WITHOUT RELIEF AND PROCEED IMMEDIATELY CHUNGKING CHINA AS COMMANDING OFFICER USS TUTUILA

After reading this the Old Man began cursing, spilling his coffee and working himself into a five-star temper. "They're sending me to Chungking on ten days' notice!" he roared. And he beat the deck with both feet, like a child in a tantrum.

Then he turned to the exec. "Call the gig away," he yelled. "And be damned quick about it!" When the gig came alongside the Old Man embarked for Manila. He stayed ashore all morning, returning to the ship for lunch.

He looked like a beaten man. "It's a lousy break," he said. "My wife cried when I told her. She loves it here. But the normal tour of duty in Chungking is a year and there's no getting out of it, so I decided to send the family back to the States."

This, I thought happily, *is really working.*

"It's unpleasant all right," the captain continued, blowing his nose with a red bandanna handkerchief, "but there are rosy sides to everything." He smiled with obvious effort. "I was lucky enough this morning to find a man with ready cash who bought my house. Matter of fact, I made $1200 profit on it." He showed us a certified check for $17,200 from a real estate agency.

"There's no Navy transport touching Manila for six weeks," the Old Man went on, "so I'm sending the family back by commercial steamer. They sail day after tomorrow on the *Jewel of Manila*." He laid four steamer tickets on the table: "The movers are coming tomorrow."

We were beginning to see that this joke had its dangers. When should we sing out "April Fool"?

The captain kept on talking. "Of course, orders is orders. But the part that burns me is the short notice. I spoke to the admiral about it, and he's sent a stinker of a message to Washington."

"The admiral did what, sir?"

"He sent a message of protest to the Chief of the Bureau of Personnel saying that my arbitrary orders to Chungking were rude and irregular and that he should have been consulted first."

My mouth felt awfully dry. The executive officer excused himself from the table. "Well," said the Old Man, "I better start packing."

I followed him to his cabin and stood in the doorway while he stuffed shirts into a suitcase. "C-c-c-captain," I finally stuttered. "About your orders—I'm the guilty party. . . ."

He interrupted me, "Of course we'll have a party! And it'll be a pistol. We can start at the Army-Navy Club, move over to the Manila Hotel. . . ."

"No, sir," I said. "You've misunderstood me. Your orders . . . to Chungking . . . they're phonies. It was an April Fool's joke. . . ."

The captain stomped across the cabin and placed his reddening face close to mine. "Mister," he said, "did I hear you right?"

"Y-y-yes, sir," I said.

He sat down suddenly on the edge of his bunk and groaned. "I've sold my house. I've made arrangements to send my family home. And the admiral is burning up the wires with mutinous messages to the Navy Department. Do you know the penalty for writing a false message?"

"Y-y-yes, sir," I said. "I can get a general court-martial."

"And that's no April Fool's joke!" Sweeney stormed. "You've really mucked things up with your grotesque sense of humor. But I'll give you a chance to straighten things out. I want to be fair."

He handed me three things: the check for $17,200, the steamship tickets for his family and a copy of the message which the admiral had sent to the Bureau of Personnel. "You go to the real estate agent," he said, "and buy my house back at no loss to me. Then go to the steamship line and get my money back on these tickets. Then go to the admiral and tell him about your little joke—and get me off the hook with him."

"Aye, aye, sir," I said.

He looked at his watch. "It's now ten to two. I'll give you until tomorrow morning to straighten things out—before I commence court-martial proceedings."

I got in the gig and went ashore. The real estate agent already had a client who had offered him $18,000 for the house.

"Look," I said. "Sell me the captain's house for the amount of this check. I'll pay you the extra $800 profit out of my own pocket. I haven't got it in cash, but I'll send you 50 bucks a month." Then I explained the situation in full and told him that if I was court-martialed I certainly would be convicted. "Okay," said the agent wearily. "Here's a receipt for the captain's check. I'll send the deed around in the morning." I smothered the guy with gratitude, ran into the street and got a taxi.

At a quarter to six I arrived at the steamship lines' offices. The man in charge said it was against rules to refund money on such short notice.

"There is only one person who can authorize it—the manager of our Far Eastern office, Mr. Gonzales."

"Where can I find him?"

"He's at the Polo Club throwing a cocktail party in honor of President Quezon and High Commissioner McNutt. About 300 guests. Mr. Gonzales is leaving for Hong Kong at six tomorrow morning."

It was eight o'clock when I arrived at the Polo Club. Guests in evening clothes were entering; an attendant at the door collected invitations. "Yes?" he questioned, eyeing my uniform.

"I'd like to see Mr. Gonzales. I have an important message for him."

"Sorry, only people with invitations—and in evening dress—may enter."

"Well, please page Mr. Gonzales then. I'll speak with him out here."

"Oh, no, *señor*," said the attendant. "Impossible."

I felt like a beggar who had been refused alms. At this miserable moment along came my friend Bessie Hackett, society editor of the Manila *Bulletin*.

"What are you doing off the *Appleby?*" she asked. I told her.

"C'mon, I've got an extra invitation at home," she said, pushing me into her car.

At home Bessie found the invitation and dragged out her brother John's evening clothes. John weighs 220 and is six feet tall. I'm five nine and weigh 150. We turned up the pants legs about a foot and pinned them in place. There was so much excess cloth around my waist that we had to fold it over—a pleated effect. The crotch of the trousers hung a few inches above my knees; the seat flopped about my thighs like an empty potato sack. The coat hung to my knees.

Within a half hour we were back at the club. The attendant, at Bessie's urging, now let me in. Everyone gaped, then laughed. The assistant manager politely informed me that entertainers were not allowed to mix with the guests. But finally I found Mr. Gonzales. I held his Martini while he scribbled out a note saying it was okay to give a refund on the four tickets.

It was now after ten and I hadn't seen the admiral yet. I changed back into uniform and taxied over to his residence, a good ten miles away. The steward who came to the door said the admiral had turned in. His orders were that he wasn't to be disturbed unless it was something official and important.

"Call the admiral," I said, drawing the steward's attention to my one gold stripe.

Eventually the admiral, putting in his false teeth and straightening his pajamas, came down. When I told him why I was there, he exploded like a 16-inch shell hitting a fuel dump. He chewed me out from rim to rim, then rushed into the next room and picked up the telephone.

"You may now go back to the *Appleby*," he said when he returned. "I've sent a message to Commander Sweeney informing him that the message to Washington has been canceled—and suggesting to him appropriate disciplinary action for you."

"Thank you, sir," I said, saluting. It was two in the morning when I got back aboard the *Appleby*. The captain was up and waiting.

"The admiral sent me a message. I know what happened there. How'd you make out on the other deals?"

I handed him the receipt for his house and showed him the note from Mr. Gonzales authorizing the return of his steamer money.

"Okay," he said in a kindly manner. Then, "Did the admiral mention the disciplinary action we've decided to take with you?"

"No, sir."

He held up some papers. "These," he said, "are the outcome of your little *faux pas* this morning. It is absolutely necessary that they get into the mail tonight. The exec and I have just looked them over, and find them in good form. But as they concern you, I want you to check them for accuracy."

"Aye, aye, sir," I said, reaching for what looked like my death warrant.

The captain went on, "The motor whaleboat will take you to the fleet post office; it's alongside now—embark and shove off. Check the papers on the way ashore. If any of the facts about you are wrong, you have my permission to change them. Now hurry," he said, handing me the papers and stamped envelopes for the papers. "The mail closes in 20 minutes."

I ran topside, leaped down the accommodation ladder and into the boat. We roared away. I switched on the battle lantern which hung under the boat canopy, and spread the papers on the seat cushion.

They consisted of three letters: one to the admiral, one to the real estate agent and one to Mr. Gonzales. Except for the addresses and salutations, they were identical:

> Thank you for your coöperation in the leg-pulling job on my Communications Officer. He went for the gag— hook, line and sinker. I've manipulated some lulus in my day; but, believe me, this is the best April Fool's joke I ever pulled.

> Sincerely,
> J. J. Sweeney
> Commanding Officer
> USS *Appleby*

Toward More Picturesque Speech I

I'ds of March

I'd like the wind to sweep a snowless path,
I'd like the rain to soothe the winter's wrath,
I'd like the sun to warm the barren earth,
I'd like spring to have an early birth.

(Talitha Botsford)

New Math

It's inflation when you have to pay $5 for the $2 haircut you used to get for $1 when you had hair

—Franklin P. Jones in *Quote Magazine*

Show Me . . .

. . . a jittery king and I'll show you a nervous rex

(Robert Fitch)

Define Lines

BUS FARE: Jack-in-the-box.

—Dick Parker

GOSSIP: Knife of the party

—Morris Bender

48

Custer's Last Stand

. . . as it might have been reported in:
Variety—"Custer Closes Out of Town"

The Wall Street Journal—"Sioux Ltd. Up 12 Points"

Pravda—"Big Red Victory"

Sports Illustrated—"Indians Win Series"

Women's Wear Daily—"Feathers Make a Comeback"
—Fred Lewis

Medical Group

Dermatologists make rash judgments

(Patricia Majewski)

Pediatricians are men of little patients

(Shelby Friedman)

NAME GAME

A GROUP of Washington State civil-service workers who jog at lunchtime call themselves "The Bureaucratic Runaround."
—Contributed by Susan M. Scott

THE SKI RESORT of Vail, Colo., has a special downstairs room for children waiting to be picked up after ski lessons. It's known as the "Bratskeller."
—Contributed by Warren Snyder

STUDENTS at Texas A & M call the university hospital the "Quack Shack."
—Contributed by Margaret C. Lawler

IN SAN JUAN BAPTISTE, CALIF., there used to be a women's clothing shop named "The Apparels of Pauline."
—Contributed by Nellie M. Gebers

Husband in Charge

By ERMA BOMBECK

I ONCE read a poll of what husbands think wives do all day long. The results were rather what you would expect.

Thirty-three percent said women spent five hours out of each day putting lint on their husbands' socks. Twenty-seven percent said they spent four hours daily pouring grease down the sink and watching it harden to give husbands something to do when they got home. A walloping 58 percent said women divided their time between watching soap operas, drinking coffee, shrinking shirt collars, discarding one sock from every pair in the drawer and lugging power tools out to the sandbox for the kids to play with.

I thought a lot about that poll, but I never mentioned it. I figured that someday . . . sometime . . . somehow . . . some man would pay for those remarks.

Some man just did.

The other day, I was summoned to Ohio to help my mother, who had had surgery and was going to be flat on her back for a few weeks.

"Are you sure you can handle things around here?" I asked my husband. "The kids, the cooking, the laundry, the whole routine?"

"Does Dean Martin know how to make a drink?" he sneered. "Of course I can handle this stuff. You just go off and do what you have to do and don't give us a thought."

I didn't give them a thought until I was paged at the airport just before my flight took off.

"One quick question," said my husband. "What does 'Bwee, no nah, noo' mean?"

50

"Who said it?"

"Whadaya mean who said it? Your baby just said it and looked kinda desperate."

"It means, 'I have to go to the bathroom.'"

"Oh. Well, that's all I needed to know. Have a good . . ."

"It also means, 'I want a cookie. Where are my coloring books? The dog just crawled in the dryer. I am floating my $20 orthopedic shoes in the john.' The child has a limited vocabulary and has to double up."

"I can handle this. It's just that she looks so miserable."

"It also means, 'It's too late for the bathroom,'" I said, and ran to catch my plane.

There was a message awaiting me at Mother's, so I called home before I unpacked.

"What's up?"

"No problem," he said cheerfully. "It's just that Maxine Milshire just called and can't drive the car pool tomorrow because she's subbing for Janice Winerod on the bowling team. She can do it today . . . unless it rains. Her convertible top won't go up. However, if the weather is decent she can trade with Jo Caldwell, who is pregnant and three weeks overdue, but who has a doctor who was weak in math. That means I will drive Thursday unless Jo Caldwell's doctor lucks out. In that case I'll have to call Caroline Seale, because I have an early meeting and it might rain. Do you understand any of this?"

"No."

"I'll call you tomorrow night."

When I answered the phone the next night, there was a brief silence. Then, "I hope you're happy. I am now the only 38-year-old boy in my office who has been exposed to German measles. And my job is in jeopardy."

"Why is your job in jeopardy?" I asked.

"Because *your* son answered the phone this morning while I was putting catsup on sandwiches and told Mr. Weems, 'Daddy can't come to the phone now. He's hitting the bottle.'"

"Tomorrow is Saturday. It'll get better," I promised.

The phone rang early Saturday.

"Hello," I answered. "This is Dial-a-Prayer."

"Oh, you're cute," he snarled. "Real cute. Just a couple of questions here. First, where are the wheels off the sweeper?"

"On the back of the bicycle in the garage."

"Check. When was the last time you were in the boys' bedroom?"

"1974."

"Check. What do you do when you have perma-scorched all the perma-press?"

"I'll be home in two days," I said.

When he didn't call me on Sunday, I called him.

"I can't talk right now," he said irritably.

"Why not? What's the matter?"

"Nothing is the matter! I bought a box of chicken for dinner, and the box caught fire in the oven."

"You're supposed to . . ."

"Don't say it. Then *your* baby chose a rather inopportune time to get a penny stuck up her nose; I've got 35 boys in the bathroom watching movies; I just tried to make a drink, and there are no ice cubes. And . . . Maxine Milshire just called to say I've been named Homeroom Mother!"

I arrived home early in the morning. My husband staggered to the door. "My wife gives at the office," he mumbled.

"I'm home," I announced. "Tell me, why is there an X chalked on the side of our house?"

He rubbed his eyes tiredly. "A baby-sitter put it there. I think we're marked for demolition."

I wandered through the house, thinking it was too late. The dog was drinking out of an ashtray. There was a pad of blank checks by the phone with messages scribbled on them. The blackboard bore a single inscription: "I am leaving, and I am not coming back. Daddy."

"Why is the baby sleeping in the bathtub?" I asked.

"She drank four glasses of water just before bedtime."

"There's a crease on your face shaped like a duck."

"I had to separate the boys, so I slept in the baby's bed."

After breakfast, my husband leaned over to kiss the boys good-by. They turned away. "He murdered our guppies!" one of them snapped.

"We'll talk about that tonight," he said.

Then he turned toward me. "Good-by, dear. You'll find everything shipshape. I mean, all you have to have is a routine. By the way," he whispered, "could you call and let me know how Lisa makes out on 'As the World Turns'?"

As I watched him leave, I thought to myself that he looked too old to be carrying a Donald Duck Thermos and a security blanket, and sporting a red rash on his neck.

HEADLINE HITS

IN THE Greenfield, Mass., *Recorder:* NUNS EXPERIMENT WITH NEW HABITS.

ON A Washington *News* story on the challenge of eating snails: WELL, THAT'S THE WAY THE ESCARGOTS

ON A Washington *Star-News* report about a music festival going on despite a court prohibition: "THE BANNED PLAYED ON."

ON A New York *Daily News* story about a cat trapped between two buildings for five hours before being rescued: "GET MEOWT!"

ON A garden column recommending composting, in the White Plains, N.Y., *Reporter Dispatch:* YOU CAN'T HAVE TOO MULCH

ON A Kansas City *Star* report on the reduction of county revenue: "COUNTY SEAT FEELS PINCH."

ON AN article in the Cleveland *Plain Dealer:* "VEGETARIANS MEET TO ESCHEW THE FAT."

ON AN article in the New York *Daily News* about the gradual conversion to the metric system: "U.S. IS PLAYING FOLLOW THE LITER."

HEADLINE in Philadelphia *Jewish Times:* "BAGEL BAKERS GET DOUGH; KNEADLESS STRIKE OFF."

ON AN Associated Press dispatch: "MASSAGE PARLORS RUB CITY OFFICIALS WRONG WAY."

IN THE ATLANTA *Journal:* "RIVER BILL UP THE CREEK."

Laughter,
the Best Medicine® II

●॥●

●॥●

AN AIRLINE pilot getting a medical checkup was asked by the doctor, "When was your last sex experience?"

The pilot said, "1955."

"So long ago?" the doctor asked.

The pilot glanced at his watch and said, "Well, it's only 21:15 now."

—Leonard Lyons

FROM the Personals column in the Roseburg, Ore., *News-Review:* "To the thief who stole the $9 hitch-coupler from my fishing-boat trailer: I send my wish that your boat breaks in half in midstream and that your mother is unsuccessful in attracting help as she runs barking along the shore."

A FRIEND of mine had just described his vacation experiences. "It sounds as if you had a great time in Texas," I observed. "But didn't you tell me you were planning to visit Colorado?"

"Well," he said, "we changed our plans because, uh..."

His wife cut in, "Oh, tell him the truth, Fred!" He fell silent and she continued, "You know, it's just ridiculous. Fred simply *will not* ask directions."

—Contributed by Dean Morgan

SAN FRANCISCO *Chronicle* columnist Herb Caen concocted a game which he calls "Punny Farm," to which readers contribute inspired names for animal pets and acquaintances. Some of the entries are: a white mouse called Mousey Tung; a collie, Flower; a boxer, Shorts; a rabbit, Transit; a donkey, Shane. A pigeon is called Toad; a frog, Horn; a horse, Greeley; and a rooster, Shire Soss. And how about a gopher named Broke; a crow, Magnon; a sparrow, Agnew; a kitten, Kaboodle; a cat, Mandu? Reversing the order, a rat is named Frank Lloyd; a collie, Melon; and a pair of egrets, Miss Otis.

APPROACHING my 40th birthday reluctantly, I called an older friend for comfort and asked, "Is it true that life begins at 40?"
"Begins to what?" she replied.
—Contributed by Joan K. Cassidy

The PR man looked at Moses in astonishment. "Moses, baby, you do it like you said—and I'll get you ten pages in the Old Testament!"
—Contributed by William W. Fitzhugh

STEPPING off a tour bus in Florence, Italy, two middle-aged American men silently studied Michelangelo's imposing sculpture, "David." After analyzing the masterpiece from all angles, one turned to the other and said, "You know, Ralph, I'll bet he could have played for the Miami Dolphins."
—Contributed by Richard A. Martens

TWO DARLING old ladies were having lunch in the dining room of a residential hotel. "I've forgotten the name of it," one of them told the waitress, "but we both want one of those appetizers my nephew bought me here last week. In a little glass you get a green olive, covered by a perfectly delightful crystal clear sauce."
—Bennett Cerf

You Can't Help
But Miss It!

●||●||●||●||●||●||●||●||●||●||●||●||●||●||●||●||●||●||●||●||●||●||●

By H. ALLEN SMITH

●||●||●||●||●||●||●||●||●||●||●||●||●||●||●||●||●||●||●||●||●||●||●

EARLY ON a May morning in 1927 Charles A. Lindbergh, flying solo from New York to Paris, saw a fishing boat in the Atlantic below him. Uncertain of his location, he throttled down, dipped his plane close to the vessel and yelled to the fishermen, "Which way is Ireland?" Later he wrote of the incident: "They just stared. Maybe they didn't hear me. Or maybe they thought I was just a crazy fool."

In my opinion Lindbergh was fortunate. If those fishermen were anything like the people I encounter from day to day, and if they had signaled directions to him, he might well have landed in Fort Lauderdale, Florida.

For all the other qualities of mind they may possess, most people, male or female, cannot properly direct a motorist or a pedestrian—or a Lindbergh in an airplane—to his destination. Several years ago my wife and I were invited to visit friends in rural Connecticut. I telephoned the lady of the house for directions. The portion of her monologue that I remember most vividly went this way: "You keep going quite a ways and finally you'll come to a three-story gray house that is burned down."

The stumbling block in that sentence would appear to be the gray house that is burned down. But there is an equally insidious semantic monstrosity: the phrase, "quite a ways." There could be a difference of 40 miles between what *she* considers "quite a ways" and what *I* consider "quite a ways." How am I to know what a farmer means when he says the next town is "a fur piece off"? Or "Not very fur"? In Latin-American countries every destination is "just beyond the next hill, *Señor*."

56

The "beyond" involved here may turn out to be 20 miles or 80 or 140.

The citizens of England have a charming but no less frustrating variation. There, when you inquire of an English countryman how to get to Popskull-on-the-Rilleragh, he will respond, "Proceed stryte ahead to the second roundabout and take the turning to the right and soon you will arrive at a cluster of small shops. Stop there, sir, and ask agayne," So you stop at the cluster of small shops and ask agayne and they send you along another few miles, advising you to stop at a certain public house and ask agayne.

The chief fault of the average direction-giver is an over-devotion to detail. "Go straight out Gutteridge," I was told in Los Angeles recently, "and finally you'll come to Division Street. Cross Division, stay right on Gutteridge. After a while you'll come to Killjoy. Cross Killjoy, keep going, stay on Gutteridge. Soon you'll see a big cemetery on a hill, then you'll come to a light—that'll be Cumshaw Boulevard. Cross Cumshaw, stay right on Gutteridge, go past a big supermarket with a red tower, just keep on going." All this drivel about cemeteries and Cumshaws and supermarkets and Killjoys could have been covered in three words: "Stay on Gutteridge." As it was, I got fouled up somewhere along the way and ended up in Oxnard.

Then there is the person, usually male and proud of his efficiency, who showers you with fractions. "Turn right at the second traffic light," he will say, "and go 7⁸⁄₁₀ miles to Hardscrabble Road. Then turn left, go 3³⁄₁₀ miles to Douglas, and turn left. Our house is exactly one tenth of a mile from that intersection." This sort of precision is likely to be the death of me: I've come within 1²⁄₁₀ inches of annihilation through keeping my attention fastened on the mileage dial rather than on the road.

Another specialist direction-giver might be called the highway-engineer type. "You go three miles on this paving block until you hit ferroconcrete," he says. "Turn left on the ferroconcrete, go four miles and then turn right on a tar job gritted with chippings. Go 2½ miles to a fork, then take the grouted macadam instead of the bituminous clinker—the one with the steep camber—and you'll come to a washboard bearing left."

This man is about as helpful as the rural nature boy who instructs the driver from the city to "keep goin' till you come to a grove of hemlocks. . . ." The city driver wouldn't know a grove of hemlocks from a pride of lions or a hand of bananas. Still, he would never confess that ignorance, so he probably ends up in a wilderness of hemlocks.

Masculine pride shows up in another way. Men will make inquiries at a filling station when lost, but they refuse to stop along the highway and ask directions of a stranger. This stubbornness has long been a source of irritation between husbands and wives. Humorist Robert Benchley once undertook to explain the wife's point of view. It is based on experience, he said, "which has taught her that *any*one knows more about things in general than her husband."

I know of a man whose business takes him by car all over the country and who would prefer death in a deep canyon to asking a stranger for directions. To this problem, however, he has found a solution. When he drives into a strange town where he has a business engagement, he finds a taxi and says to the driver, "Go to 1564 Hickory Street." Then he simply trails along after the cab.

In the art of direction-giving I would naturally like to point to myself as a paragon of efficiency. I know how it should be done. If you live in a difficult locality and find it necessary to tell people how to get to your place, rehearse your speech. Make it simple, and make it crystal-clear. Don't clutter it up with bituminous clinkers or three-story gray houses that are burned down.

But will mankind profit by this hard-earned advice? Of course not. We'll all blunder along like the woman I know who asked an Iowa farmer how to get to a certain town. He gave her a long routine of turn rights and bear lefts and finished off by saying, "You can't help but miss it!"

Cat With a
Telephone Number

By FRED SPARKS

IT'S A HUMILIATING confession for a bachelor to make, but whenever my phone rings the call most likely concerns not me but my cat, name of Stoop. We live, Stoop and I, in a New York apartment one flight up. The branch of an oak tree brushes the railing of our back terrace, providing a feline staircase that enables Stoop to live a double life—civilized and sedentary within the apartment, completely uninhibited when he climbs down the tree and prowls the outside world.

I first met Stoop three years ago. I was walking home on a bitterly cold night when I saw a tangerine-red kitten sitting on a snowy brownstone stoop. As I approached, the creature tried to stand, wobbled, then fell down a step, half-frozen.

I wrapped the few ounces of shivering fur in my scarf and got an immediate purr of confidence. At home, Stoop (an obvious christening) responded immediately to an eyedropper-feeding of warm milk lightly laced with brandy. Within a week he was frisking around my place, and by spring, thanks to the spreading oak tree, he had discovered the exotic world of New York's sidewalks.

When his excursions lasted longer and longer, I bought a light collar and had a tag inscribed:

> THIS IS NOT A STRAY.
> IN EMERGENCY PHONE
> FRED SPARKS BU 8———

Unlike full-time alley cats, who flee anything on two legs, Stoop is trusting. As he wanders through the neighborhood, strangers stop to pet him. Attracted by the tag, dozens of them have phoned me. They seem under the impression that Stoop has run away or was lost. They sound disappointed when I assure them that he can find his own way home.

A gentleman I hadn't seen in years called up and said, "Well, well, it *is* a small world. I stop to pet a cat and find you're back in town. Remember that $20 you owe me?"

That wasn't the only time Stoop was expensive. One caller identified himself as the owner of a seafood restaurant down the block. He complained that cats had been raiding his kitchen through a basement window, filching crabs and lobsters. "The only one I could catch had this telephone number," he said. "Please give me your address. I'm going to send you a bill for his share."

I obliged, convinced it was a joke. As I walked away from the phone something crunched under my shoe. A lobster claw.

By the time Stoop had been on the streets for six months, he was a combat veteran of the cement jungle. His nose was crisscrossed with scratches, and his ears were nicked with notches like a Western badman's belt. But in spite of the horrendous things that supposedly happen to small animals loose in the big city, he shows no evidence of ever having been mistreated. In fact, many of the phone calls come from friendly souls who want to be sure of doing the right thing. "I've got your nice cat with me in a phone booth," a man said recently. "Is he allowed to eat a fig?" Another wanted to know if Stoop could safely handle lamb-chop bones.

The wife of a U.N. delegate phoned one Sunday to report that Stoop was a guest at a garden party in her nearby town house. "He just strolled in and is now having an anchovy," she said. "Won't you join us?" I did, and it was a lovely party.

Stoop certainly gets around. One morning he climbed into a cab parked down the street. I heard about it when an excited voice on the phone asked, "You-the-guy-widda-cat?" When I said I was, he rattled on, "Holy smoke! I'm a taxi driver and I thought I'd seen everything. But when I got in line at Grand Central Station, I find this cat sitting in the back seat. With a telephone number, yet!"

"Where is he now?" I asked, apprehensively.

"In a coin locker. Pick up the key at the starter's office and leave me the quarter. And say, Mister! How about a tip or something? Nobody—not even a cat—is supposed to ride free."

Stoop gets around locally, too. A call came late at night, a few months ago, from an indignant female. "Your *cat* is under my bed!" she snapped. "I got a look at his tag before he ran away from me and hid."

Trying to calm her down, I said, "How do know that it's a he?"

"Because he's been corrupting *my* cat, a *her*."

Curtly she gave me her name, Helen —————, and her address, a ground-floor apartment across the yard. When I went over to collect my housebreaking cat, I tried to apologize for his bad manners, but she slammed the door on both of us.

Two nights later it happened again. This time I brought along a box of chocolates for Helen and a catnip mouse for her tortoise-shell pet. She found this amusing, and I found her really an attractive girl. We agreed to have dinner together.

Stoop doesn't see Helen's cat any more. But I still see Helen. Now when the phone rings, I know that at least sometimes it's for me.

CAUGHT IN PASSING

TEACHER watching fireworks display: "I once had a class like that."

—Contributed by LeRoy J. Hebert

DIETING woman: "I'm almost down to what I didn't want to get up to."

—Contributed by Alyce L. Humphrey

AT A group-sensitivity session: "The way I look at it, self-pity is better than none."

—Arnold H. Glasow

DURING a political discussion: "Which side of the fence are you straddling?"

—Contributed by Georgianna E. Smith

AT A Washington, D.C., cocktail party: "If there's anything I can't stand, it's a blame-dropper."

—Contributed by Angie Papadakis

Diet Tribe

"I warned you about those nutty
crash-reducing programs, Martha."

WEAVER IN *THE WALL STREET JOURNAL*

"At long last my diet is having an effect.
Now I can see the numbers."
BOB BARNES, REGISTER AND TRIBUNE SYNDICATE

"And when you open the door
the speaker says, 'Hello, Fatso!'"
SHIRVANIAN, GATES FEATURES

© CHON DAY

"You don't eat them. Just spill them on the floor three times a day, and pick them up one at a time."

BERNHARDT, MASTERS AGENCY

Oh, Say, Can You Ski?

By COREY FORD

YOU MIGHT NOT suspect it, but you are face to face with one of the world's foremost indoor skiers. I've conquered the far-flung slopes of Canada and the Alps by the simple method of skiing sitting down, usually with a glass balanced in one hand. Just let some other skier start to tell me about *his* conquests, and I'm off on my rocking-chair runners in a cloud of artificial snow.

My breath-taking triumphs on the hickories (as we old pros call them) are all the more remarkable because I don't know a *sitzmark* from a hole in the ground. Frankly, winter sports leave me cold. Why climb a mountain at 20 below zero when you can fall downstairs in a nice warm house?

It's my idea that winter is a good time to catch up on your sleep. Nobody went outdoors in the old days. People used to board up the windows and sit around the fire playing parcheesi or doing card tricks until spring. That is probably why they lived longer then. At least, it seemed longer.

Not any more, though. The first snowfall is the cue to rush out, strap the waxed boards on top of the car and head for the frozen trails. Slalom courses crisscross the suburban landscape, ski-tows creak up every incline of more than ten degrees, and snow buses beat it back to the city on Sunday night, full of amateur *schussboomers* with bloodshot eyes, a pair of frost-bitten ears and one arm in a sling.

Not that I have any objection to people who ski, provided they shut the door behind them when they go out. What I object to is the social stigma which attaches these days to people who don't. Winter is hard enough without facing the taunts of those enthusiasts who insist on dragging you off for a robust weekend upside down in six feet of snow. "Come on, you old fogy," they jeer. "Get some red roses in those cheeks. Put on the barrel staves and let's try a few *geländesprungs.*"

Travel posters add their seductive siren-songs. "Visit our winter wonderland at beautiful Mount Traction," they urge, "complete with emergency first-aid stations, 24—hour stretcher service, and a fully equipped modern hospital conveniently located at the bottom of the hill." Even the family joins in the assault. "Why don't you let Junior take you out to the children's slope this afternoon?" your wife suggests pointedly. "He can hold your hand in case you get going too fast."

There's only one way to maintain your self-respect as a red-blooded male, and still avoid getting snow down your neck—take up indoor skiing. All you need is a few hours under a sun lamp, the names of several prominent mountain ranges, and a smattering of German phrases like *"Ski heil!"* and *"Prosit!"* It also helps if you can yodel.

The first step is to purchase a pair of skis. This involves a trip to a sporting-goods store, but you can avoid undue exertion by taking a taxi, and the clerk will be glad to stoop over and fasten the bindings for you if you can't reach them. Walk up and down the floor a couple of times, just to make sure the skis fit. If they are the right length, the curved points of the tips will just coincide with your forehead as you fall forward. When you have made your selection, break them across your knee, carry the pieces home, and hang the shattered ends over your mantel with a small sign reading "Splint's Ledge, Feb. 22, 1957." The rest of the skis can be used to start a fire.

Next you'll need a complete ski outfit. Naturally your clothing should be imported, so you can drape your jacket carelessly across a chair with the foreign manufacturer's name exposed. In case nobody notices it, pick up somebody else's jacket and remark apologetically: "Say, I guess I got hold of the wrong one—mine had an Innsbruck label."

Now for the real snow job. Armed with dark glasses, sun-tan lotion and a plaster cast on one leg (just in case somebody asks you to ski), hie yourself north to a popular resort. Take a chairlift to the top of the mountain and stretch out on a chaise longue in the glass-enclosed sun deck. This is one of the best places to practice indoor skiing, because the chances are that nobody else knows any more about it than you do.

The trick is to break in on another skier's story. Let us say that an expert is expounding his pet theory on how to take the downhill slalom. Interrupt with some lighthearted quip like: "Speaking of slalom, I took one in Newfoundland that went 20 pounds." (I admit this isn't very good, but anything to throw him off stride for a moment.)

Expert *(recovering)*: As I was saying, it's all in distributing your weight properly. You should lean slightly forward—

You: Except in Chile. Everybody leans backward down there because it's on the other side of the equator. I suppose you're familiar with the big jump at Satan's Sacroiliac?

Expert: Well, no, I've never been in South America.

You: Oh, that's not in South America, that's in the Alps. *(Craftily.)* Personally I think the Alps have it all over Switzerland, don't you?

Expert *(walking right into it):* I thought that Switzerland was *in* the Alps.

You: I mean the Himalayan Alps, of course. *(This is what I mean about keeping him off balance.)* You haven't been skiing until you've gone down Devil's Abdomen, or Old Nick's Adam's Apple. Have you ever run the Apple?

Expert *(weakly):* I'm not exactly sure where—

You: Never forget the time I took it blindfold on a dare. Glare ice, you know, and what made it even harder was the fact that I lost one ski when I hit a mountain goat. Fortunately I caught up with a snowslide going in the same direction, and rode it the rest of the way down. . . . Wait a minute, please don't go. I want to tell you about doing Hell's Handbasket with both feet tied behind me. . . . Do you really have to leave?

By this time all the other skiers will have departed as well, and you can ride the chair lift back to the bottom of the mountain, full of the buoyant spirits and ruddy glow of health that an afternoon of indoor skiing gives.

Parlez-Vous Pixie?

By JACK WOHL

Goblins, Go Home!

By WILL STANTON

EVER NOTICE the way Halloween has been going downhill? Used to be great time for kids. Tip things over. Throw stuff around. Not anymore. They put on costumes, collect candy bars, bubble gum. End of fun. Damn shame.

Decided to do something about it. Explained to Maggie, my wife. "Oh, my God!" she observed. Only harmless pranks, I told her. Soap windows. Throw rotten tomatoes. Maggie said where do you find rotten tomatoes? Good point. Told her we'd use fresh ones. She said at 49 cents a pound why not just throw money? Dropped subject. Didn't forget it.

Halloween. Offered to take boys, Roy and Sammy, into town. Good place for trick or treat. Maggie suspicious. Boys eager. Roy dressed as clown. Sammy as pirate. Plastic pails. Identification tag on each costume. My name—address— phone number. Good thinking.

Parked car in middle of block. Let kids collect treats. Last house, man gave them pumpkin jack-o-lantern. I told them enough treats. Time for tricks. Gave each a bar of soap to draw on windows with. Skull and crossbones—scarecrows. Kids came back, said couldn't reach windows. Always excuses.

Moved on. Sammy said don't forget pumpkin. I hadn't. Hoped he had. Forty pounds and slippery. Also carrying Roy's hat and Sammy's mask. Stopped at house, gave boys pins to stick in doorbell. No doorbell. Next house same deal. Looked around. No garbage cans. Asked boys what they'd like to do. Said go to bathroom. Told them wait until we got home. No dice.

Problem of walking up to strange house—ask to use bathroom. Couldn't do it. Woman could. Man no. Can't explain.

Looked around. Neon light in distance. Emil's Bar and Grill. Told boys follow me. Any port in storm. Pretty ratty-looking port. Showed kids men's room. Put pails on bar. Also hat, mask, pumpkin. Ordered drink. Hate to use men's room without buying something.

Solitary drinker couple of stools away. Red face, necktie loose. Heard him speak to bartender—Emil. Pointed remark about big kid not satisfied with one pail, spoil it for all the others. Emil brought drink. Asked which pail I wanted it in. Told him never mind the comedy. Red-faced man moved over, asked if I minded personal question. "How come you're wearing pirate mask with clown hat? What the hell you supposed to be?"

Didn't know what was keeping boys. Sounded to me like somebody outside was singing hymns. Women's voices. Emil looked at watch. Said, "Starting early tonight." He could hear them too. Glad of that. Emil explained. Group of church ladies trying to get saloon closed. Picketed place every evening. Sang hymns. Passed out tracts. Recalled reading about it in paper.

Boys came out of the rest room, ready to go. Told them no rush. Put them on stools. Ordered ginger ale for them. Reviewed situation. Militant ladies outside singing "Rock of Ages." Bad time to walk out of saloon with two children. Unfavorable impressions. Somebody bound to recognize me. Only one solution. Put on mask and clown hat. Gave boys pails. Picked up pumpkin. Said let's step lively. Outside, mask fell off. Singing stopped. Ladies stared. Flash bulb went off—man from local paper. More flash bulbs, comments from ladies. Left in quiet dignified manner.

Suggested going home but boys wanted more trick or treats. Said they'd meet me at the car. Let them go. Went around corner to car. Not there. Possibly not right place. Tried next block. Other blocks. Checked all pirates and clowns. Not many out, raining too hard. Time for decisive action. Call Maggie. Ask her what to do.

Went up to house. Rang bell. Asked man if I could use phone. Man said well he'd be a son of a gun. Woman called out who was it. "Pagliacci," man called back. I'd forgotten about clown hat. "I'll hold your pumpkin," he said indicating phone in hall.

Maggie answered. "What happened?" she asked. "The boys said you were supposed to meet them at the car." I said, "You mean Roy and Sammy?" She said yes, those were the ones she meant. "When you didn't show up they telephoned and I borrowed the Jacksons' car and drove into town and picked them up."

Told her it was slight misunderstanding. Asked her where she had picked them up. Precisely. Told her I'd be right home.

Found car okay. Home. Boys still up. Maggie looked at me. Closed her eyes. Asked what caused all the foam. Told her not foam—soapsuds. "While the boys were waiting by the car they soaped the windshield. Had to drive all the way home with my head out the window. What with the rain and the soap—"

Maggie said I must be proud of the boys. Chips off the old block. Voice sounded unnatural. Strained. Told her soaping the family windows didn't count. Supposed to play pranks on others, not on own family. Roy said they did. In the rest room at the bar. Threw toilet paper around. Wrote on mirror.

Told Roy he hadn't learned to write yet. Said no, but he had learned to print. Copied his identification tag on mirror. My name. My address.

Roy said how come my face looked so funny? Glanced in mirror. Dye from wet clown hat. Orange streaks from forehead to chin. Maggie said don't annoy the tiger, and took kids upstairs. Poured myself a drink. Poured two. One might spill.

Maggie came downstairs. "You were right about Halloween," she said. "I never really appreciated it before. The way the boys were talking made me realize there was something special about it—a sort of magic."

She had a point. How else was I going to explain my picture in the paper, coming out of a saloon with two small boys? Wearing clown hat. Carrying pumpkin. Ladies in background singing hymns.

"Magic is the only word," I said.

Life in These United States® II

●‖●●

●‖●●

A FAMILY drove into a vacant campsite. The children exploded from the car and began feverishly to assist in every possible way to make camp. They were fast and efficient, and soon the tent was up, the ice chest unloaded, firewood gathered, and the sleeping bags were in place. Then the children disappeared. When a nearby camper commented on this superlative display of teamwork, the father explained, "I have a system. No one goes to the rest room until camp has been set up."

—Stuart Lassetter *(Ames, Iowa)*

MY HUSBAND, an inspector in the building-construction industry, sometimes inspects the steelwork on skyscrapers in the New York area, where many of the workers on the high steel are American Indians.

When the first column on the last floor is erected, it is customary to raise the American flag on a pole affixed to the column. After the day's work, a party is held below, with free sandwiches and beverages. While my husband was working at a building under construction in the financial district, another building was going up two blocks away. It was time for the topping-out festivities, and the Indians invited their brother tribesmen on the nearby structure to join them. How was the invitation extended? By smoke signals—made with the smoke from the forges used to heat the rivets.

—Herta Lonlax *(Astoria, N.Y.)*

A BACHELOR friend, moving to a house in the suburbs, rented a panel truck, into which he loaded his books and furniture.

73

Arriving at the house, he drove the truck into the connecting garage and unloaded it. Once the weight was off the springs, however, the vehicle became taller than the top of the garage door by several inches; he couldn't get it out. So he went around the neighborhood and asked all the housewives, their husbands, even the postman to come and stand in the truck. With their combined weight, the truck was lowered enough to be moved out.

In one hilarious session, he got to know his neighbors and established himself as a fellow who needs help—and he has received a steady supply of cookies and cake ever since.

—Arch Napier *(Albuquerque, N.M.)*

I WAS having an unprofitable evening at the racetrack. In the first three races my $10 horses had run third, fifth and second. I noticed that a dapper-looking elderly man near me was having a good night. He cashed winning mutuels on the next four races, while I continued my cold streak.

Finally, the feature race! I decided I would bet the way he bet. I gave my girl my last $2 and asked her to follow this horse-betting genius and latch onto whatever he latched onto. One minute before post time, she returned. Smiling broadly, she handed me two roast-beef sandwiches and a beer.

—Michael J. Sparren *(Ilion, N.Y.)*

THE MORNING after my operation, though I was barely conscious, my nurse insisted on changing me from the hospital gown to one of my own. She brushed my hair, powdered my face, added a touch of lipstick. Stepping back, she surveyed me with satisfaction. "There!" she said, and added confidentially, "Dr. Culpepper simply *hates* to see his patients look sick."

—Mrs. Milton W. Edwards *(Collins, Miss.)*

AS A school principal, I accompanied a group of kindergartners to the circus. The balloon man came to our area, and one little girl frantically waved her hand to attract his attention, then asked the price of the balloons. "Fifty cents," he replied. She dug into her tiny pocketbook and finally displayed a quarter. As she put the coin in his hand, he explained to her that she would need another quarter. She took back the quarter, tucked it into her purse and searched out another one. With a satisfied look, she again put a quarter in his hand.

The balloon man realized that he had met his match. "You win, honey," he said. "Keep the balloon."
> —Richard K. Ocker *(Carlisle, Pa.)*

WE WERE taking a drive in the country when we spotted a large white banner staked on the front lawn of a farmhouse. In bright letters it proclaimed: "Free Martini With Each Kitten."
> —William F. Simmonds *(Mentor, Ohio)*;
> James C. Bryan *(Cuyahoga Falls, Ohio)*

A FRIEND of mine often goes fishing with a business associate who owns a large boat. Returning to port one afternoon, they discussed their longing for a lobster dinner and bemoaned the fact that the market would be closed before they could get there.

Approaching the harbor, they found themselves in a field of lobster buoys. Suddenly, the skipper turned off the engine, leaned over, grabbed a buoy and pulled the pot aboard. Inside were two fine lobsters. As he extracted them, my friend suggested that this was an improper procedure, since they couldn't very well leave payment in the bottom of the ocean. After a moment's thought, the skipper went below and reappeared with a bottle of 12-year-old Scotch. He wrapped it in a plastic bag, pushed it into the lobster pot and tossed the pot overboard.
> —Robert Bennink *(Cambridge, Mass.)*

THE MALE population of our office was visibly impressed— and shaken—by the arrival of curvaceous Rita, a new member of the secretarial pool. (Her desk, strategically close to the coffee machine, increased consumption and profits noticeably.)

One morning, my office door burst open. There stood Harvey, a middle-aged appreciator of life's finer things. "My gawd, Dick!" he exclaimed, his eyes wide. "You should see Rita today. She's wearing a *see-blue throusel!*"
> —Richard N. Whittington *(Glendale, Mo.)*

I BECOME somewhat excited at my son's high-school football games. One night, when he made a particularly good tackle, I punched the person next to me and loudly proclaimed, "That's my son who made that tackle."

"I know," she replied quietly. "He's my son too."
> —Lyle Clark *(Indianapolis, Ind.)*

Now That I Understand Golf

●II●II●II●II●II●II●II●II●II●II●II●II●II●II●II●II●II●II●II●II●II●II●

By GRAHAM PORTER

●II●II●II●II●II●II●II●II●II●II●II●II●II●II●II●II●II●II●II●II●II●II●

I LAY AWAKE in the midnight darkness. That day, for the first time in my personal golfing history, I had broken 90. I nudged my sleeping wife. "Can you believe it?" I cried. "I'm no longer a duffer! The secret of golf is simply . . ."

". . . a matter of beginning your downswing with your shoulders instead of your hands."

"How did you know?" I asked, amazed.

"Because that's what you've been muttering all night," she sighed. "Don't you think you should get some sleep now?"

She was right. In a few hours I would play my first-round match in the club tournament against my arch golfing enemy, Steve Galloway. I chuckled into my pillow sadistically. With the secret of the game now locked in my breast, I would humble him at last.

I shut my eyes and ordered my mind to go blank. It insisted, instead, that I replay each stroke of my day's round. During the first two holes my smile all but illuminated the night shadows of the room. But when I found myself again missing that 20-inch putt on the third green, my smile turned itself off. That putt had hurt. So had the four other short ones I muffed later on. If I had sunk them, as I surely would in the future, I would have completed my round in 84. And if one of my drives hadn't sliced out of bounds, costing me two strokes, I would have toured the course in a sizzling 82.

Or might I not have scored better still? The supposition caused me to gasp aloud, waking my wife with a start. Now that she was no longer asleep, I could find no reason for not sharing my joyous discovery.

"I had some tough breaks not of my own doing today," I explained. "A perfect pitch to the ninth green took an astounding hop into a bunker. My drive on the 12th freakishly scooted beneath a bramblebush. And on the 17th my caddie sneezed at the top of my backswing, all but causing me to miss the ball completely. Since those were obviously non-recurrable accidents, wouldn't you agree that . . ."

"Why is it," my wife interrupted, "that a man can recall for a week every single shot of his last game, but can't remember for five minutes that the screen door needs fixing?"

I lay back in a pretense of sudden sleep. But my subconscious refused to accept the sham. It kept busy subtracting those last three strokes from my hypothetical round of 82. When I arrived at the amazing figure of 79, my body seemed to float toward the ceiling. *"Good Lord!"* I cried. *"I'm a championship golfer!"*

Every shred of evidence now pointed to my being able to par even the toughest holes on the course. And should it be my good fortune to slip in an occasional birdie—and, after all, why shouldn't I?—well, the implications were downright staggering.

Ever so carefully, so as not to cause my wife to phone a psychiatrist, I slithered from bed and gripped an imaginary driver. For a moment I waggled it in delicious anticipation. Then, powerfully and smoothly, I swept my body through an entire swing. Had the siutation been born in reality, the ball would surely have zoomed into orbit. I drew in my stomach and threw out my chest and, in the utter darkness of the bedroom, exuded more confidence than ever before in my life.

Confidence! *That* was the key—confidence born of my new mastery of technique. How incredible to realize that in all these years I had simply conducted an endless series of tiger hunts on the golf course, violently beating the earth with my clubs, exhausting myself with my very ineptness. But tomorrow would be different. Poor, unsuspecting Galloway!

At 2 A.M. I begged my mind to let me sleep. My plea was in vain. By three o'clock I had won the club championship. An hour later I captured the U.S. Open. Dawn was creeping over the windowsill before I divested myself of an armful of phantom trophies and tumbled into a canyon of sleep.

MY WIFE and I and the Galloways sat together on the golf-club terrace, watching the sun call it another day on the fickle fortunes of man. Now that my tournament match was over, I wished I were alone, like Napoleon on Elba. Not even on Boy Scout timber hikes had I seen so many trees. No doubt about it, I would have scored better with an ax.

Without looking up, I felt the sting of Steve Galloway's glance. This time, I decided, I was giving up golf for good. While my wife talked, I gazed out over the fairways, which the evening dew had tinted with silver. On either side, the terrible, towering trees now slept, harmless and serene. It seemed impossible to believe that this gentle, pastoral scene had earlier proved itself such a violent battlefield.

I downed my drink, and somehow it made me feel better. My eyes were drawn back to the lush, quiet fairways. The course was beckoning me now in the shadows. "Come," it seemed to whisper. "Conquer me."

As I refilled my glass, I began feeling surprisingly relaxed. Much the same as I had felt yesterday when I shot my 89.

Ah, so *that* was it—*relaxation!* Not how you pivoted your hips or snapped your wrists, but simply how well you relaxed! No wonder Galloway had trounced me so completely; my mind had been gorged with a jumble of mechanical do's and don'ts. By taking it smooth and easy, wouldn't those technical elements fall naturally into place? Yes, yes, I saw it clearly now. After years of huffing and puffing on the links, I had got the message at last.

Almost breathlessly, I stared out over the golf course, lost in wild surmise. What, I wondered, should I wear while competing in the British Open? A touch of heather, perhaps? I could only hope I would not be so relaxed as to drop my trophy on the toe of the Queen. I tried not to sound condescending as I turned to Steve Galloway. "How about a return match next Saturday?" I asked.

"But, darling," my wife protested, "that's when you promised to fix the screen door."

For a moment her words buzzed near my ears like mosquitoes, then mercifully took flight when Galloway's voice led him to slaughter: "Ready for another licking, eh?"

I only smiled in the dark. Already I was growing joyfully tense, just contemplating the wonders of relaxation.

Strong Medicine
For Careless Guests

●‖●

By PARKE CUMMINGS

●‖●

WHEN FRIENDS visit us in our house in the country they're apt to leave various articles behind when they depart, after which they write and ask me to mail them back to them. None of them ever repeats this offense, however. I am allergic to wrapping up stuff and lugging it to the post office, and I have devised a system to break them of this careless and irritating habit.

What I do is cheerfully coöperate. Let me illustrate with how I handled Ed Hamilton, who left a pair of shoes after a weekend last October. The minute I received his request to mail them I answered.

October 18

Dear Ed: Got your letter. I was wondering how you could have left your shoes behind. Did you go home barefoot? I hadn't noticed. Parke

Ed replied that he hadn't gone home barefoot. He had taken an extra pair of shoes, and he wanted me to mail them to him. Again I coöperated.

November 7

Dear Ed: I'm all set to send those shoes back to you, but first I've got to know which pair you left here, the ones you were wearing when you arrived or the extra pair you brought along? Parke

Ed wrote back, demanding, for Pete's sake, what difference

did it make whether he left the pair he was wearing or the spare pair? He wanted those shoes. My own reply was considerably more courteous.

> November 23
> Dear Ed: The reason I asked was because I wanted to know what color the shoes were. Please let me know, because I want to return them to you *at once*. Hope your family is feeling fit.   Parke

The next letter from Ed struck me as a bit abrupt. It just said "Brown."

After I recovered from a cold that had laid me up I promptly wrote him another letter.

> December 17
> Dear Ed: Now we're getting somewhere! I figured they were either brown or black, and it's good to know definitely. The shoes are as good as yours. Just tell me where you left them and I'll send them without delay. Best wishes to you and the family for Christmas.   Parke

Soon afterward I received another letter: "In the guest room, stupid! Where else?" Not a word of Christmas greeting from him. However, I ignored this rudeness when I next wrote.

> January 11
> Dear Ed: Great news! I found your shoes. Size 10½, eh? Don't bother to confirm this, as I want to get them off to you without a moment's unnecessary delay. Unfortunately I mislaid your earlier letters and I forget whether you want me to send them by railway express or parcel post.
>   Parke

In his reply Ed said he didn't give a damn how I sent them just as long as I got those shoes off in a hurry.

As soon as I could, I wrote him back.

> February 18
> Dear Ed: It sure looks as though you'd be receiving those shoes any day now. I've decided on parcel post. Do you want me to mark "Fragile"? Please give me this information so I can get them off promptly. Warmest regards to you and all your lovely family.   Parke

Shortly afterward I got a wire from Ed saying, "Quit stalling and send those shoes."

A few days ago I actually mailed them. My guess is that Ed will be less apt to leave his property behind when he makes future visits, and the same holds true of other guests with whom I have coöperated. And it's highly gratifying to know that I've never once addressed a single unkind word to any of them.

REMEMBER WHEN...

... it was people who were coöperative instead of apartment houses.

—Robert Orben

... "freeze-dried" meant the family laundry had hung all day on the clothesline.

—Beth Rickels

Have You a Pash
for Ogden Nash?

●‖●

●‖●

OGDEN NASH, *the late American comic poet laureate, delighted thousands with his uncurbed doggerel. Here are choice examples of Ogden Nashery.*

Some tortures are physical and some are mental,
But one that's both is dental.
> —New York *Journal-American*

THE PERFECT HUSBAND

He tells you when you've got on too much lipstick,
And helps you with your girdle when your
hipstick.
> —*Versus* (Little, Brown)

Whenever poets want to give you the
idea that something is particularly
meek and mild,
They compare it to a child,
Thereby proving that though poets
with poetry may be rife
They don't know the facts of life.
> —*The Saturday Evening Post*

The trouble with a kitten is THAT
Eventually it becomes a CAT.
> —*The Saturday Evening Post*

Poets aren't very useful,
Because they aren't very consumeful or very produceful.
—The Saturday Evening Post

Sometimes with secret pride I sigh
To think how tolerant am I;
Then wonder which is really mine:
Tolerance or a rubber spine?
—The Saturday Evening Post

Breakfast foods grow odder and odder;
It's a wise child that knows its fodder.
—Redbook

Celery, raw,
Develops the jaw,
But celery, stewed,
Is more quietly chewed.
—The Saturday Evening Post

The one-l lama,   And I will bet
He's a priest.   A silk pajama
The two-l llama,   There isn't any
He's a beast.   three-l lllama.

(The author's attention has been called to a type of conflagration known
as the three-alarmer. Pooh!)
—London Clubmen Magazine

I regret that before people can be
    reformed they have to be
    sinners,
And that before you have pianists in
    the family you have to have
    beginners.
—The Saturday Evening Post

The parsnip, children, I repeat,
Is simply an anemic beet.
Some people call the parsnip edible;
Myself, I find this claim incredible.
—The Saturday Evening Post

In the Dark

ANGIE PAPADAKIS

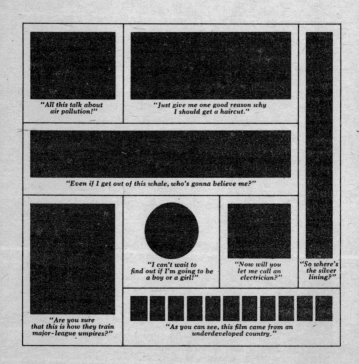

"All this talk about air pollution!"

"Just give me one good reason why I should get a haircut."

"Even if I get out of this whale, who's gonna believe me?"

"I can't wait to find out if I'm going to be a boy or a girl!"

"Now will you let me call an electrician?"

"So where's the silver lining?"

"Are you sure that this is how they train major-league umpires?"

"As you can see, this film came from an underdeveloped country."

Mona Sue and
the '39 De Soto

●||●||●||●||●||●||●||●||●||●||●||●||●||●||●||●||●||●||●||●||●||●||●||●

By LARRY BATSON

●||●||●||●||●||●||●||●||●||●||●||●||●||●||●||●||●||●||●||●||●||●||●||●

MONA SUE COOPER had hair as black as six feet up a smokestack and a shape that could bring tears to your eyes. We linemen on the school football team used to elbow one another when she walked past us in the hall, then turn in quiet desperation and bite off the nearest doorknob.

She was the best-looking girl in high school—with the exception of Mary Elizabeth Ables, who dated only quarterbacks. (Just to clear up the point, we lived far enough south so that all the girls and most of the boys used two front names.)

Mona Sue played the drum in the school marching band and was on display at all home games and some of those in nearby towns. I pinned my hopes on the road games.

It was the amiable—and economical—custom of our football coach, Bullet, to permit team members of good character to drive their own or their parents' cars to nearby games. Not infrequently, enough players did this to enable Bullet to dispense with hiring a bus.

My plan had the simplicity of Bonaparte's more successful campaigns. I had become owner of a '39 De Soto coupe. I would establish myself with Bullet as a lad of strong moral fiber, obtain permission to drive to a road game, then ask Mona Sue to ride back with me. Riding *back* was the key. Under school rules she would have to take the band bus to the game. But it wasn't unheard of for one of the band girls—a girl of spirit—to drive home with her swain.

It took several weeks to bring Bullet around. I called him "Sir," asked questions in my most sincere manner and yelled,

"Darn right!" every time he made a point. Still there was only the game at Mountain view left when Bullet caved in.

Mona Sue capitulated when I cunningly asked her whether her bandmates would be shocked.

After the game, I was a blur of motion from field to locker room to my car, where Mona Sue waited.

With her drum.

Her bass drum would not fit into the trunk of my '39 De Soto. The only place it would go was right in the middle of the seat, provided the driver and his passenger each scrunched painfully against a door handle. Conversation was possible, of course, but driver and passenger couldn't see each other, much less do anything else.

The night was young, and worse lay ahead. After the engine warmed up, I switched on the heater. Slowly a nauseating, unbearable stench filled the car. I stopped and checked everything but couldn't find the source. It was a little better if we switched off the heater, but after another mile or so we had to roll down the windows. Our hands and feet grew numb.

We had 25 miles to cover, and the first 15 passed in silence. Then I croaked inanely, "You there?"

"Oh, God, am I ever!" Mona Sue replied.

As we neared town, I suggested that hot chocolate at the Cinderella Confectionery might thaw us out. "Why don't you get some after you take me home!" Mona Sue snapped.

The next day she told everyone in school that I had been hauling hogs to market in my car. She began dating Jerry Lee Smith, who had unlimited use of his father's pickup. They later married.

Some time afterward, Jerry Lee confessed that he had smeared Limburger cheese all over the manifold and heater of my car.

And, 15 years after I left home, Mary Elizabeth Ables told my sister that she'd always been interested in me but I'd never given her a tumble.

All in a Day's Work I

●●●

●●●

ALONG with the usual sticks of gum and squashed candies, my two young trick-or-treaters came home Halloween night with something a little different in their sacks. In orange cellophane, neatly tied with black ribbon, was a packet of homemade treats—a candied apple, a couple of cookies, a square of nut fudge—and this typewritten note: "Grandmotherly, cookie-making type, will baby-sit, in this neighborhood, for a reasonable fee."

—Contributed by Mrs. J. L. Gallagher

A FRIEND of mine in the bookkeeping department of a small firm locates and pulls ledger cards for posting. Her job title is simply "puller." One day her daughter reported that her second-grade class had been discussing their parents' occupations. "Mommy," she said proudly, "the teacher was more interested in your job than in anyone else's." My friend asked why. "I don't know," chirped the tot. "All I said was you were a pusher."

—Contributed by Jane Wesely

WHILE we were covering, for the Canadian Broadcasting Corp., the crowning and enthronement of a new Patriarch of the Russian Orthodox Church in Moscow's Yelokhovsky Cathedral, my cameraman discovered he'd forgotten his black film-changing bag. Unable to unload and reload the film in the light, we faced the prospect of missing the enthronement ceremony, which was about to begin.

A nearby priest noticed our dilemma. Without a word, he

pushed the film magazine under the heavy black folds of his robe, and nodded to the startled cameraman to make the necessary film switch. The new roll of film was ready within minutes—in time to catch the most important part of the ceremony.

—Contributed by Ab Douglas

AN accountant won an office pool, and he was asked if he would report his winnings to the IRS. Before he could answer, a co-worker interjected: "He won't even report this to the MRS!"

—Contributed by Randy W. Ingalls

OUR firm, having moved into a new building, celebrated with an open house, serving cocktails and hors d'oeuvres to 600 guests. The bash lasted long into the evening. The next morning I looked at the guest book and found that, on the last page, the two janitors had signed their names, and added the comment: "Incredible mess!"

—Contributed by Sherri J. David

THE management of a motel called a plumber when a cat somehow got in between floors where the plumbing system is located. The man who came didn't do any actual plumbing work, but he had to account for his time, so he submitted this bill:

$12.50—Called "Kitty-Kitty"
125 times @ ten cents a call.

—Contributed by W. H. McDaniel

A FORMER airline hostess, I was on my first deluxe bus trip, and I was amazed at the services offered. Included were meals en route, rest rooms, public-address announcements and a uniformed hostess. I introduced myself to the hostess, and we compared notes on air and ground travel.

At lunchtime, she gave out menus offering a choice of sandwiches. As she began filling orders, a problem arose. There weren't enough egg-salad sandwiches. She rushed up front and whispered to the driver, who pulled to a halt. A similar bus traveling behind us also stopped. Our hostess dashed to the other bus and soon returned with a batch of egg-salad sandwiches. As she passed my seat, she asked, "Could you do *that* on a plane?"

—Contributed by Barbara L. Jack

Confessions of a
Little League Coach

●Ⅱ●

By JOHN G. HUBBELL

●Ⅱ●

ONE NIGHT just before my first season as a Little League coach, I proclaimed my bold approach to the task ahead. I wasn't going to be like those other Little League fathers. No, sir! "I've read about those guys," I informed my wife. "Besides over-organizing everything, they put too much emphasis on winning. They've taken the game away from the kids, made emotional wrecks of them."

"You're perfectly right, dear," she agreed. "I think you definitely should get everything disorganized and see that the boys lose a lot."

"That's not what I meant!" I yelled calmly. "I meant that when I was a kid we just found ourselves a stick and a ball and a vacant lot. We turned out some pretty good ballplayers, if I say so myself, and we learned the most important thing of all—sportsmanship."

That's how I conceived my job: to see that the boys on my team all had a good time and learned sportsmanship—and a little something about baseball. But people continued, in the days ahead, to misunderstand me.

At the coaches' organization meeting, the league president handed out rulebooks and schedules, then asked if there were any questions. I had read a lot about over-competitive coaches who, in their desire to win, cut their least talented players from the squad. I had strong feelings against this practice, and here was an opportunity to express them. "About this business of cutting players," I began.

The president turned lobster-red. "I don't know where *you* have been coaching," he said. "But we don't cut *any* kids in our league. If a boy wants to play, he *plays*—at least half of each game. Let's get that straight right *now!*"

"But that's what I . . ."

"Winning isn't *everything!*" someone hissed.

"Good," I said weakly, sitting down. "That's fine."

Then there was the business with the T-shirts. This was little Little League, sort of a Little League farm league, and my kids were all under eight. When they were issued bright-green T-shirts with white letters proclaiming them the "Cubs," their delight knew no bounds. In a few days my spouse informed me, however, that my shortstop—my pride, my joy, my son—refused to remove his T-shirt for any reason. "He even sleeps in it," she complained. "It's *filthy!* You must speak to him!"

"My mission," I said, "is to see that the boys have a good time and learn sportsmanship. It is their mothers who must keep them sanitary."

But I was misunderstood again. Other mothers with the same problem insisted that *I* had a certain responsibility in this matter of cleanliness. "We're all in this together," they said. Thus it was decided that on Saturday mornings the Cubs would travel en masse to a coin laundry to have their shirts cleaned; and it was "only logical" that the coach, whom the kids "looked up to," should lead these expeditions.

I actually began to enjoy the weekly challenge of keeping 15 half-naked Cubs from tearing up the laundry—but it made the proprietor nervous. "I fast and pray all day on Friday, and go to bed at sundown," he said. "Please take them someplace else."

"Not a chance," I said. "We're all in this together."

Practice was now in progress, and we had some eventful ones. I had got my second baseman, who fielded ground balls well, to think about trying to throw the runner out at first instead of holding the ball high and loudly calling attention to his proficiency. And my first baseman had largely overcome an aversion to covering his post when a runner was bearing down on it. But my son was still playing shortstop sidesaddle. "You've got to get *behind* those grounders," I told him. "It puts you in position to throw."

"What if the ball hops and hits me in the face?" he asked.

"Have you ever seen Zoilo Versalles reach for them like you do?"

"I'm not Versalles," he said. "I'm just a seven-year-old kid trying to learn a little . . ."

"Get behind them!" I explained.

Then came our first game—with the Giants. My lads went to bat first. My lead-off batter, Davy, was 42 inches high and absolutely fearless. To be sure, there was little to fear from the opposing pitcher; his deliveries, which followed a high, lazy arc, had the catcher ambling to all sides of home plate. As the count reached three balls and no strikes, I noticed that Davy was becoming increasingly agitated. "Whyncha throw it somewheres nearda plate, ya jerk?" he inquired.

"Shaddup, ya runt!" the pitcher replied.

As the next pitch headed for the stands, Davy scurried out of the batter's box, pushed the catcher sprawling and timed his swing beautifully. *Pow!* He sent a hot grounder straight at the petrified enemy third baseman. The ball streaked untouched through this unworthy's legs and came to rest midway between him and the left fielder, who showed no inclination to involve himself in the situation.

Davy rounded first base and, to the ecstatic shrieks of his teammates, was making for second. But now the catcher had regained his feet and was heading crosscountry toward Davy, obviously bent on vengeance. As Davy dived into second, the catcher dived on top of him. They struggled around in a thickening cloud of dust, out of which Davy suddenly appeared running toward third. By this time, the left fielder had been persuaded to pick up the ball, and he now heaved it mightily toward home plate, where there was no one home to catch it. Davy bounded home amid much cheering and backpatting by his teammates. "Davy hit a *homer!*" they shrieked.

Above their clamor, the opposing coach was bellowing, *"Illegal! Illegal!"* He danced toward me, waving his finger at Davy. "He can't slug my catcher! What are you *teaching* your kids, anyway?" He turned to the crowd of mothers and fathers behind his bench. "He'd do *anything* to win! He's the one at the coaches' meeting who wanted to *cut* . . ."

"Listen, buddy," I said, sticking my jaw up in his face. My kids were crowding noisily behind me. I heard Davy yell,

"Give it to him, coach! Nice guys finish last!"

This unsportsmanlike observation recalled me to my senses, and the umpire, an experienced man with a large voice, restored order. Davy's run was not counted, and he was lectured sternly for his unseemly sentiments.

The rules in our league state that a team shall remain at bat until there are three outs or until nine players have batted. So, when the Giant pitcher walked the eight Cub batters who followed Davy, we took the field for the bottom of the first inning with a comfortable five-run lead. We fattened this as the game progressed; in fact, we went into the bottom of the fifth and final inning with an eight-run bulge—26–18.

This last half inning proved to be big. My pitcher walked the first two batters and hit the third, loading the bases. Then a husky lad lofted a fly ball to center field. My center fielder got under it, but at the last possible moment he removed himself from harm's way, letting the ball drop and roll to a stop. At this point, he pounced on it and began running with it toward the infield. My shortstop ran to meet him, shouting, "Lemme have it! I'll relay it!"

"*I* wanna relay it!" the center fielder yelled, running past him. The shortstop took after him, leaped on his back and beat him to the ground. Meanwhile, four runs scored.

The next Giant batter grounded one toward my third baseman, who came up with it beautifully—and threw the ball into right field. A series of similar catastrophes followed, and in a few minutes the game ended with the Giants on top, 27–26. Our opponents gave three big cheers for the Cubs. I had some difficulty getting my stalwarts to reciprocate, but finally wrung three weak cheers out of them for the Giants—followed by Davy's departing insult: "You guys really *stink!*"

"We beat you bums!" one of the Giants pointed out.

"Yah, wait'll next time," my shortstop yelled. "We'll *cream-ya!*"

It did seem, as the season progressed, that next time we might cream them. My Cubs took off on a long winning streak. All the parents turned out in support. "Kill the umpire! Get him a seeing-eye dog!" they would shout.

As the season waned, we continued winning. What bothered me, though, was that the opposing coaches kept yelling to the umpires to make sure that I played all my players, not just my best nine. ("He's the one at the coaches' meeting who...")

This began to wear me down. "Listen, buddy!" I would shrill, charging at them. "Well, all *right,*" they would say, "you don't need to get so up*set* about it. After all, it's only a *game.*"

We won our park championship. Then, in the district championship game, we lost, 16–15. I was gloomy. To my astonishment, the Cubs were not; they had done their best and had no apologies to make to anyone. Without even being told to, they gave three lusty cheers for their conquerors. It made me feel good, and I knew they had learned something big when Davy yelled, "Nice game, you guys. Ya beat us fair 'n' square. But wait'll next year!"

"Yah," I shouted at the opposing coach, "wait till next year! We'll *creamya!*" I could tell from the man's face that I had been understood at last.

PUN-IN-CHEEK

"THAT'S what I like," remarked a cocktail-party guest when the hostess brough in a tray of hors d'oeuvres. "The platter of little treats around the house."

—Contributed by Ronald Bert

WE WERE searching for a stopping place after a hard day of driving. "There *was* a motel back there," sighed my mother wistfully, "but that was *neons* ago!"

—Contributed by Selma Raskin

Art Buchwald's
"Abnormal" Relationship

By ART BUCHWALD

LAST WEEK I celebrated my seventh wedding anniversary. I'm not bragging—as a matter of fact it was a very disturbing thing. When I looked around, I discovered that many of my friends who were married around the same time are either separated or divorced. There were so few who were still happily married that I decided there was something wrong with us.

"We're sick," I said to my wife. "What's happened to us?"

She agreed. "We're abnormal. Everyone is talking. Most of the girls I went to school with have been married at least twice."

"For the last seven years we've been drifting together," I said. "I think we need some outside help."

"I was going to say the same thing," she said. "I'm willing to seek it out if you are."

It was good to clear the air, and we immediately made an appointment with a divorce counselor. A divorce counselor operates like a marriage counselor except, instead of trying to get people together, he tries to break them apart. Most people go to a divorce counselor only as a last resort, when it looks like the marriage is going to last forever.

We arrived at his office together. This was our first mistake. The receptionist asked us to enter separately. The reception room was simply furnished with chairs and a low table with magazines featuring stories such as "Wedding Bells Drove Me Mad," "My Secretary Made a Better Wife Than My Wife Made a Secretary," and "How I Invested My Alimony and Made a Million Dollars."

The counselor came out and nodded to us to come in.

We sat down and the first thing he said was: "I'd appreciate it if you didn't hold hands in this office."

We put our hands on our laps.

"Now tell me your story and don't leave out any details. A thing that may seem unimportant to you could shed a great deal of light on the case for me."

We told him everything, how we had met, about our home, how, although we had occasional fights, we always made up.

He kept tapping his pencil against his ear.

"Do you have any arguments about money?" he asked.

"No," I said. "I give it to her and she spends it."

He frowned.

"Now, when you have a fight, does she ever threaten to go home to her mother?"

My wife replied, "My mother lives too far to go home and, besides, the children are in school, and I hate to have them miss a term."

"Do you ever send your wife flowers?"

"All the time," I replied. "I get them wholesale."

"Does he notice when you go to the hairdresser or when you buy a new dress or hat?"

My wife said, "Oh, yes. I can't buy anything new without his commenting on it."

"What does he say?"

"He wants to know how much it cost."

"And when you tell him does he get mad?" the counselor asked hopefully.

"No, he just shrugs his shoulders and walks into another room."

The counselor broke his pencil in half.

"Do you have things in common to talk about?"

"Oh, yes," I said. "Lots of things."

"Like what?"

"All our friends are breaking up."

"What about your girl friends?" he said to my wife. "Do they ever call you up and tell you they saw your husband having lunch with a beautiful girl?"

"Oh, yes," my wife said. "But that's his job. If he didn't talk to beautiful women at lunch I wouldn't be able to buy any new clothes."

The counselor threw the broken pencil across the room.

"This is the most hopeless case I've ever tackled. Why don't both of you grow down? Everything you've told me makes no sense at all. You have too much in common. My advice to both of you is as follows: Go home and try to get on each other's nerves.

"You must learn to be a jealous wife," he said to my wife. "And you have to show a little more immaturity," he said to me. "Keep track of each other's faults. Blow up little things until they seem like big problems. Move into smaller quarters; infringe on each other's thoughts. Remember this—love and happiness aren't everything."

I thanked him profusely as he escorted us to the door. But when I opened the door for my wife he blew up.

"For heaven's sake!" he screamed. "You're not even out of my office and you're already opening doors for her. How are you *ever* going to break up if you keep doing stupid things like that?"

BOOK MARKS

HAROLD H. MARTIN gave a copy of his book to his dentist, with the inscription: "To Dr. W, the greatest worker in gold since Benvenuto Cellini."

—Contributed by Mrs. Dixon Preston

WINSTON CHURCHILL gave Franklin D. Roosevelt a copy of one of his books, with this message on the flyleaf: "Another fresh egg from the faithful hen."

FERNANDES GARVIN dedicated her book *The Art of French Cooking:* "To Jan, my husband, because there are no men like the ones his mother used to make."

Laughter, the Best Medicine®III

●‖●

●‖●

A YOUNG fellow, suffering from insomnia, decided to see a doctor. "Count to ten and repeat it until your eyelids feel heavy," advised the doctor. A few days later, the sufferer returned to the doctor's office. "You seem the worse for wear," said the physician.

The young man explained that it was the effect of the advice. "I count," he said. "But when I reach eight I always jump out of bed."

"Why?" asked the doctor.

"I'm a boxer," he replied.

—Contributed by Arsene Rakotovao

FOREIGNERS in Tokyo have been chuckling over the announcement at the entrance of a new restaurant. The establishment is the last word in continental elegance, with an army of waiters impeccably dressed in evening clothes and a wine steward in festooned jacket and knee breeches.

The neatly printed English-language announcement reads: "To Our Distinguished Guests—Please be assured that the vegetables used in the preparation of the fine French dishes in our new restaurant have been washed in water personally passed by our chef."

—Contributed by D. M.

A YOUNG woman had given birth in the elevator of a North Carolina hospital, and was embarrassed about it. One of the nurses, in an effort to console her, said, "Don't feel bad. Why, only two years ago a lady delivered in the front yard of the hospital."

With that, the new mother burst out crying. "I know," she wailed. "That was me, too."

—Contributed by Vernon T. Hearn

A FEW years ago, while employed as a secretary for a research laboratory, I was required to obtain security clearance from the office of the Chief of Naval Operations. After completing the necessary papers, I was advised to make arrangements with our local police department for fingerprinting.

Entering the police station the following afternoon, I found a good-looking young man at the front desk. I walked up briskly, smiled fetchingly and said, "Hi! Can you take care of my Naval inspection?"

The young officer blushed and quickly replied, "I'd be happy to accommodate you, ma'am. But they only let me take fingerprints."

—Contributed by Nadine H. Kerr

AS THE Israelite leader stood on the shore of the Red Sea with his people gathered around him, a horde of Egyptian soldiers rushed toward them with banners flying and swords flashing in the sun. The public-relations man edged up to him and said, "Moses, baby, what are you going to do now?"

"Raise my arms like this," Moses replied, "and when I separate them, the waters will roll back and we will cross to the other side."

Glancing at the rapidly approaching Egyptians, the PR man pressed further. "What will you do then?"

"I'll wait till the Egyptians are halfway across," said Moses. "Then I'll raise my arms again and the waters will close, engulfing and destroying our enemies."

The PR man looked at Moses in astonishment. "Moses, baby, you do it like you said—and I'll get you ten pages in the Old Testament!"

—Contributed by William W. Fitzhugh

SPECIAL SERVICE

A FEW years ago I received from the Eastman Kodak Co. some processed film, with a letter explaining that it had been sent to them without the owner's name and address. By projecting the film, they had been able to make out the license number on a car appearing in one picture, had checked with the state motor-vehicle bureau, had traced the car to me and sent the pictures in the hope that I could identify the person who took them. It was my brother.

—Contributed by Ruth Jackson

RECENTLY we received a bill for a pair of sneakers from a shoe store in St. Johnsbury, Vt., where our daughter is attending school. The following handwritten message was added: "Charged by your daughter. She tells me she misses you all and will be quite glad to get back home. School is going nicely. The Management."

—Contributed by Katherine K. Hart

SALLY'S mother-in-law, recently arrived from Italy, loved to shop. But in her part of the world no thrifty housewife would dream of paying the first price asked. Sally was deeply embarrassed to discover her mother-in-law haggling with the neighborhood grocer. The vegetables didn't look fresh! The fruit was ready to rot! Surely he wasn't going to ask such a price!

The grocer, also Italian and a very understanding man, solved the problem. He regularly gave the old lady a good fight, and lost. Then once a month he sent Sally's husband a bill for the difference.

—Contributed by Lorna Slocombe

Droodles!

●||●||●||●||●||●||●||●||●||●||●||●||●||●||●||●||●||●||●||●||●||●||●||●

By ROGER PRICE

●||●||●||●||●||●||●||●||●||●||●||●||●||●||●||●||●||●||●||●||●||●||●||●

A droodle is a drawing that doesn't make sense—until you know its correct title. Take the example to the left. This may appear to be meaningless, but it isn't. It is called "A Ship Arriving Too Late to Save a Drowning Witch."

Try your hand at titling the following droodles. Answers follow.

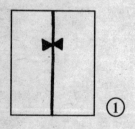

①

②

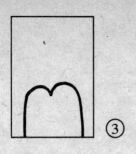

③

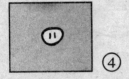

④

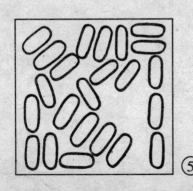

⑤

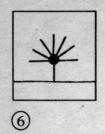

⑥

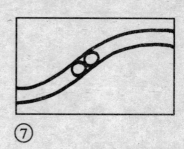

⑦

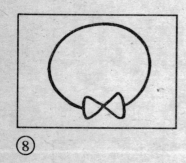

⑧

⑨

Answers to Droodles

1. Man in Tuxedo Who Stood Too Close to Front of an Elevator
2. Fat Man Smoking Pipe in Soft Bed
3. Nudist Looking for a Collar Button
4. Pig Emerging From a Fog Bank
5. Aerial View of Used-Bathtub Lot
6. Spider doing a Handstand
7. Two Corpuscles Who Loved in Vein
8. Butterfly Skipping Rope
9. Pieces of Eight
10. Inside view of Napoleon's Coat
11. Three Degrees Below Zero

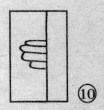

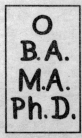

The French Correction

●■●

By LAWRENCE ELLIOTT

●■●

MY WIFE speaks fluent French and has always assumed that, with a little effort, so could anyone else in the Western world. I grew up in Brooklyn, where even ordinary English comes disguised as a foreign language, so you can see the potential for woe. We married, nonetheless, for better or for worse—and with Gisèle's assurance that a little painless bedtime conversation would have my fractured high-school French up on its feet in no time. *Vive la France!*

Alas, if you have ever tried to teach your mate to play golf or drive a car, you know there are some things even consenting adults, especially married ones, shouldn't do. One word led to another, few of which I ever wholly grasped—for example, she called me *une bête*, which I understood to mean a beaut but turned out to be a beast—and our noble experiment was over.

Then, three years ago, our son Nicholas was born, and I had to come out of linguistic retirement. One day Gisèle rushed home from the library to announce that a baby's mind was a *tabula rasa*. I took this to be Italian for red table wine and asked if she was sure. "I just spent two hours researching it," she said forcefully. "A child has no preconceived ideas, no resistance to learning, no inhibitions. So we can teach Nicholas two languages as easily as one."

"But he's only 11 days old."

"Exactly the time to start."

Before the day was out, The Plan was fully operative. Gisèle

104

was cooing to him exclusively in French while, from Chaucer to Charlie Brown, his English instruction was entrusted to me. What he was destined to speak to us only the omnilingual *Dieu* knew. *Vive la Tour Eiffel!*

In the beginning, *Le Dieu* was compassionate. When Gisèle cradled Nicholas in her arms and crooned, *"Cher petit enfant; oh, mon beau garçon!,"* I followed the drift pretty well (Dear small infant; oh, my handsome waiter). And of course Nicholas' earliest contributions to the conversation, nerve-jangling wails most often loosed around 3 A.M., were simple enough to understand.

Then came his first real word. It was in French—"Pa-pa"— and I was exuberant; this is going to be easy, I thought. It was so easy that I began encroaching on Gisèle's domain. For some reason she objected to this. She said something about my mangling the French language, but I think her real concern was that I'd get so good at the old *parlez-vous* that Nicholas wouldn't learn any English. Anyway, I certainly impressed our friend Richard. *"Va chercher votre tractor green and show it to Ree-chard"* (Go seek out your green tractor and show it to Richard), I would say.

"I didn't know that you spoke French," Richard would say.

"Don't encourage him," Gisèle would say.

But again one word led to another, Nicholas this time stringing them together to form French sentences. "What did he say?" I kept asking, and quite often Gisèle would reply, "He said he had to go to the bathroom. But never mind—it's too late."

In self-defense, I kept a French dictionary by my side, but do you know how long it takes to look up *salle de bains* (bathroom)?

Gisèle asked me would I be offended if we taught Nicholas to come to her with certain requirements. I said not to worry about me. *Vive la guillotine.*

Eventually Nicholas learned that chances of a fruitful dialogue were enhanced if he addressed me in English, but the insidious convolutions of French grammar had already left an indelible mark on both of us. Strolling in town one spring day, he said to me, "Take off the sweater of me."

"You just keep on the sweater of you," I insisted. "It makes cold."

"I have warm."

"Look, Papa has on the sweater of him. All the people have on the sweaters of them. The wind cold, he blows on us." I noticed that some passers-by had stopped to stare, so I took off the sweater of him and we moved on.

That night I sat brooding about the capriciousness of the French. Wasn't it typical that the words they used to describe something always came after the something? Wasn't it ridiculous—the tractor green, indeed! Then why did I keep talking that way?

Enter my son, the bilinguist. "What you making?" he asked.

"I'm not making anything," I said. Then it dawned on me that this time it was French parsimony that was blocking the channels of communication. Their verb *faire* was forced to do the duty of "to make" as well as "to do." "You mean, what am I *doing?*" I explained triumphantly.

"What you doing?"

"Nothing."

"Papa not make nothing."

"Papa not make *any*thing," I corrected testily.

Nicholas, puzzled: "What you say me?"

Papa, undone: "I say you that I not *make* nothing. I *do* anything!"

By now, the attentive reader will have noted that I am highly suggestible. And it got worse. I began having corkscrew nightmares in which an endless line of tractors wound through an immense field pulling their colors behind them. By day I sounded as though I had swallowed but not digested a French vocabulary list.

Then there came the time, as it must to all fathers, when Nicholas was committed to my care for an entire day: Gisèle was off to New York City on a shopping expedition. She had seen to our welfare: "I've left potato-and-leek soup on the stove for lunch; all you have to do is heat it. I'll be home to get dinner."

The train came and she was gone, and Nicholas and I returned alone to that big house in the country to grapple with the old communications barrier.

"You are the papa of the mama of me?" he asked for starters.

"No, I am the husband of your mama," I answered reasonably. *"Je suis le*—how do you say 'husband' in French?"

"Mari."

"Je suis le mari de ta maman."

He studied me darkly. I wondered if the scrutiny in his brown eyes reflected my conviction that, in French, everything seems faintly illicit. But all he wanted to know was who was the husband of him. By the time we straightened that out, it was almost time for lunch. I lighted the stove and set the table.

Suddenly Nicholas came barreling into the kitchen spewing French like a runaway oil well. *"Oh, Papa! Le chien de Monsieur Levy lit notre journal!"* I believe this translates into, "The dog of Mr. Levy is reading our newspaper," but perhaps not. In any case, we had had enough experience with the dog of Mr. Levy, our neighbor, so that I was more than willing to investigate. What the hound was actually doing was spreading our newspaper all over our front lawn, creating confetti as he went.

I chased the dog and Nicholas chased me, squealing with delight. I had not seen him so happy since the washing machine backed up and flooded the basement. And the dog, of course, ran into the house through the open door. I followed a trail of overturned vases and muddy paw prints, finally cornered him under a table and escorted him out. Then I sank into a chair, *très fatigué,* and contemplated the wreckage.

"Papa," my little French scholar came in to announce, *"le potage est en train de bouillir."*

"I don't understand—the pottery is on a broken train?"

"Non, non! C'est le potage—il est en train de bouillir."

He wandered off, only to return ten minutes later with the story. Wearily I opened the French dictionary and began, laboriously, to work it out: the-soup-is-in-the-act-of-boiling-over. I bolted for the kitchen.

Actually, the soup was all finished boiling over—over the stove, the walls and the floor. There was none left in the blackened pot.

"I have hungry," Nicholas said.

"I have hungry, too, kid. Let's head for McDonald's."

That evening, he was full of excitement when we picked up Gisèle at the railroad station. *"Maman, j'ai mangé un gros hamburg-aire et beaucoup de pommes frites."* (Mama, I ate a giant hamburg-aire and many French fries.)

"What about the potato-and-leek soup?" Gisèle asked me.

"It's a story long," I said. "If you promise not to ask about it, I'll promise to take a French course for beginners."

Well, we both kept our word, and the only thing to add is that I am the star of my class. After all, how many beginning French students dream of tractors green and have all the home instruction they can cope with? *Vive la French toast!*

HOW'S THAT AGAIN?

FROM the DuPage County, Ill., *Times:* "The committee approved a resolution allowing James and three other committee members to go to Springfield and discuss the possibility of stocking lakes with state conservation officials."

FROM the New Haven, Conn., *Register:* "Even if you don't carry perfume flacons with you, you can smell sweet all day and night if you saturate a bit of cotton with your favorite scent and tuck it into your bra. The scene will remain active for almost 24 hours."

REAL-ESTATE ad in the Aiken, S.C., *Standard and Review:* "Unusual home with fireplace, carpeted living room-dining room combination, and fully equipped kitchen which can be closed off with shudders."

FROM the Sherman County, Ore., *Journal:* "The Legion Auxiliary met on Tuesday. The principal business was that of arranging pippies for the annual poopy sale."

FROM the Rochester, N.Y., *Times-Union:* "Attention is shifting to the Senate itself, where opponents have promised an allpout filibuster."

FROM the Fort Worth *Star-Telegram:* "The Congressman sat informally on the thick carpet and discussed food prices and the high cost of living with several women."

Hello, Dali!

By WILL STANTON

AWHILE BACK, a fellow was telling me about a new form called
a happening. What you do is get some people to dance and
somebody to read poetry. Get somebody else to splash paint
on the wall and on the dancers and the poet. Scatter some
seaweed around if you have any. That's about it. Art is everywhere. Trouble is—we don't always recognize it.

Decided to make some wine a while back. Squeezed the
grapes and put juice in a jug with sugar and yeast. Too much
yeast maybe. Put the jug on top of the freezer out of the way.
That was Friday. Next morning my wife, Maggie, said I'd better
do something. Went out to the kitchen.

Stuff had started to work during the night. Purple foam was
coming out of the jug, down the freezer, across the floor. Place
smelled like abandoned fruit stand. Gnats all over, lurching
and reeling. Took jug into bathroom and put it in the tub.

Maggie had to do some shopping. Told me to look after the
kids. Said I would. My daughter Kit was wearing a hair drier
and practicing the guitar. Not easy. Roy and Sammy, the two
youngest, were watching TV. Terrible picture. Fellow was
supposed to come and fix it.

Looked out the window. Sammy asked what I was looking
at. Told him nothing. Asked me if I'd almost seen a squirrel.
Said yes. Anything to shut him up. Didn't work. Asked me
how many people I knew. Told him 42. Asked me who they
were. Told him Fred. Who else? Ursula. Who else? Said that
was all I could remember.

Roy wanted to know if he could use a rolling pin. Asked

109

him what for. Said he wanted to roll out modeling clay. Told him to use a bottle out of the trash.

Went into the bathroom to check on the wine. Cat in the tub playing with the foam. Tried to catch it but couldn't. Cat went through living room. Left purple paw prints on the rug. All the way across.

Fellow came about the TV. Poked around. Said probably antenna was out of adjustment. Asked me to watch picture and tell him when it looked better. Said he'd holler when ready. Told him to call down through the chimney. Noticed the fireplace needed cleaning out. Got the wheelbarrow to put ashes in. Changed my mind and decided to do something about the rug.

Got pail of water and started to wash out paw prints. No dice. Sammy kicked the bucket over. Soaked whole side of the rug. Wasn't going to do the floor any good, either. Lifted edge of rug and shoved wheelbarrow under it to keep it off the floor and let it dry. Put the hair drier on top of it and turned it on. Couldn't do any harm.

Roy said there was a lady at the door. Turned out to be old school chum of Maggie's. Harriet something or other. "I've been wanting to meet you and your wonderful family for ages," she said.

Told her Maggie ought to be back soon. Harriet got part way into the living room and stopped. Said, "Oh."

"Cat ran across the rug," I explained. Roy had left the bottle on the floor. Gin bottle. Put it in wastebasket. Told Harriet to sit down.

"I can just as well come back later," she said, "I don't want to disturb you." Told her I hadn't been doing anything. Turned off sound on TV. Left picture on. Harriet sat on edge of chair. Knees together. Hands clasped.

Sammy said, "My dad almost saw a squirrel."

Harriet jumped. Said, "That's nice, dear." Not much of a conversationalist.

Kit came in with the guitar. Introduced her to Harriet. "When are you going to take the wine out of the bathtub?" she asked. Told her there was no rush. "I want to take a bath," she said. Told her should have thought of that when she washed her hair. Harriet waved her hand, brushing off gnats.

Sammy said, "My dad knows 42 people." Harriet smiled. Lots of teeth.

Sammy said, "He can only remember the names of two of them."

Harriet said, "Oh?" Limited vocabulary. Fixed smile. Still fighting the gnats.

Sun came out. Mentioned it to Harriet. Small talk. Put her at ease.

"Yes," she said, "it looked like rain earlier, but I think it's clearing up."

TV picture faded and came back sharp and bright.

"Excuse me." Went over and yelled up chimney. "That's fine. Hold it right there."

Voice answered. Hollow sounding. "I thought that would clear it up. Be right down." Turned around. Harriet gone. Flighty sort of woman.

Maggie came home and saw the rug. Looked thoughtful. Mentioned Harriet to her. Kids all got in two cents' worth. Took about an hour.

Maggie leaned back on couch. Eyes closed. "Harriet was one of my best friends," she said. "What will she tell people?"

Very little, was my guess.

"I was only gone a short time," she said. "How could all this have happened?"

Suddenly all was clear. A happening. A work of art had taken place right in our house. Explained to Maggie. Maggie said, "Don't speak to me."

Hasn't spoken to me yet. No buttons on shirts. Holes in socks. Cold toast. No matter. Beauty is everywhere. Art will endure.

MATTER OF CONSCIENCE

There is only one way to achieve happiness on this
    terrestrial ball,
And that is to have either a clear conscience, or none at all.
                —New York *Journal-American*

Innocents Abroad

"Some of these places must have cost a fortune to heat."
HANDELSMAN IN *PUNCH*, ENGLAND

"I wish you wouldn't try to order in French."
GALLAGHER IN *THE SATURDAY EVENING POST*

"What does Daddy mean—act nonchalant?"
REAMER KELLER, KING FEATURES

"Like the guide book says, it can be done!... I'm doing Europe on $5 a day!... The other $45 is being spent by my wife!"

"—and so we say a fond farewell to four thousand six hundred eighty dollars and fifty-five cents."

Relics From the
20th Century

●○●
By PIERRE BERTON
●○●

A recent archeological expedition to the former site of New York, one of the ancient cities of the Old World, has been highly successful. The excavations, painstakingly carried out over a three-year period, have produced many new artifacts which cast further light on the lives of the primitive people who inhabited this area in the mid-20th century. Reproductions of some of the chief finds are shown below:

Note the classic lines, simple and yet authoritative, of this roadside god, whose effigy appeared at regular intervals along thoroughfares of the day. Natives propitiated the deity by regular offerings of small metal pieces on which had been carved, with great ingenuity, the face of their leader or chieftain.

Cunningly wrought from preserved skins of domestic animals, this fetish was carried everywhere by the males of the tribe, who believed that its possession conferred good fortune upon them. Without it, they felt lost, almost naked. Its presence gave them a sense of power and confidence, and a feeling of "belonging."

Twentieth-century man's ideas of the working of the human body were crude in the extreme. Here is a 1960 conception of what the human brain was like. Natives actually believed that little hammers inside the head caused headaches, tension, edginess, etc. They often swallowed pills in the hope of combating this "dull feeling."

Hand-carved clubs of various styles, many of them beautifully wrought, were chief weapons of the period. Tribes fought with them incessantly, and even children were drawn into warfare. Circular object (right) came equipped with string so that it could be retrieved by user after enemy was bested.

The researchers had great difficulty identifying this object, believing as they did that by the early 1960's all cooking was done within the dwelling. As these and similar artifacts were always found in the backyard or native *patio,* they concluded that the objects were used for animal sacrifices to the various gods of the day. The theory is fortified by discovery of heavily charred bones in the near vicinity.

These beautifully designed garments (*aprons*) are believed to have been worn by holy men presiding at sacrificial rites. Animal juices staining many samples reinforce the theory. Note the delicacy of the workmanship and the sophistication of the native drawings, which show high ability and a fundamental understanding of both art and taste. The natives were obviously highly developed in such skills and handicrafts.

Life in These United States® III

●Ю●Ю●Ю●Ю●Ю●Ю●Ю●Ю●Ю●Ю●Ю●Ю●Ю●Ю●Ю●Ю●Ю●Ю●Ю●

●Ю●Ю●Ю●Ю●Ю●Ю●Ю●Ю●Ю●Ю●Ю●Ю●Ю●Ю●Ю●Ю●Ю●Ю●Ю●

RETURNING to New York on an ocean liner, I became friendly with a group of Irish immigrants on their way to various parts of the United States. As the ship approached the Manhattan skyline, one country lad gazed in astonishment at the long line of morning traffic on the West Side Drive. "Sure now," he gasped, "will you look at the size of that funeral!"
—Edmund G. Carroll *(Baldwin, N.Y.)*

WHILE traveling in Vermont, my husband and I stopped at a small general store in a quiet village to replenish our supplies. After an unsuccessful search of the shelves for canned baby foods, I asked the proprietor for assistance. "You see," he said, "I heard about this population explosion and decided not to carry any baby foods. The next store's 45 miles away, and it sorta makes folks around here think twice before doing anything unnecessary."
—M.B. Hutchinson *(Laconia, N.H.)*

WHILE driving through Tucson at about 2 A.M., I noticed the tail lights of a distant car weaving slowly from one side to the other of the nearly deserted freeway. Considering the hour, I concluded that the driver had just been flushed out of one of the local cantinas, and I began to plan how I would ease past him.

Approaching cautiously, I was surprised to see that the car bore the markings of the Arizona Highway Patrol. But as I passed, my confidence was restored. Just ahead of the patrol car was a huge red Hereford steer, sauntering nonchalantly along, being herded expertly toward the nearest off-ramp.

—Irwin M. Newell *(Riverside, Calif.)*

MY FRIEND Ann has a jewel of a cleaning woman. Every Wednesday morning, right after Ann's husband and three children have left for the day, Mrs. Olson appears and cheerfully plunges into her tasks until three, just before the children return to a sparkling home. Ann's husband and the children are enchanted by the stories Ann tells of the warm, homely philosophies of Mrs. Olson. She has practically become an unseen member of the family.

As a matter of fact, she is just that. Every Wednesday afternoon at three, Mrs. Olson removes her cleaning clothes, collects the $15 Ann's husband has left for her and regains her own identity—that of a young housewife and mother, $15 richer, named Ann.

—Pat Brown *(Tarzana, Calif.)*

A WEST VIRGINIAN worked at a factory in a neighboring state. Telling his co-workers about a forthcoming trip back to his native state, he said, "Martha and me are repairin' to go on a little vacation back to West Virginny."

A fellow worker interrupted, "You mean you're *pre*paring to go on a trip, not repairing. To repair means to fix something."

"That's what I said," retorted the mountaineer. "We're fixin' to go."

—Jack Land *(Warren, Ohio)*

SHORTLY after my wife and I moved into a large apartment building, I decided that I would take advantage of our sixth-floor location to work on my "shape-up" program.

Each day after work I would spurn the luxury of the elevator and jog up the stairs. I soon discovered that my business clothes made me too warm, so I would shed my coat and tie at the bottom of the stairs and begin unbuttoning my shirt as I went up.

One day, on the third-floor landing, I met an elderly couple who gave me a curious look. As I went by them, the husband turned to his wife and, nodding knowingly, said, "Newlyweds."

—Frank Russell *(Anchorage, Alaska)*

WAITING for the traffic light to change, I noticed an automobile that had stopped for the light, but not until it had completely blocked the crosswalk. A stream of pedestrians was forced to single-file around the front of the car, while exchanging dirty looks with the driver. One young woman had a better idea. In passing, she hesitated a moment, then reached down and pulled the hood release, raising the front end of the hood about three feet. She scampered on her way just as the light changed again.

—E. R. Fitzgerald *(Soap Lake, Wash.)*

ON A LATE summer afternoon, the bus pulled to a stop across from a supermarket. There was a bicycle leaning against the bus-stop sign, and a man carrying a watermelon in his arms came to the bus door. He explained that he had just bought the melon but found he couldn't handle it on his bike. Would the driver deliver it to a corner about 2½ miles down the road? The driver reluctantly agreed, but warned that he would not be able to wait for the man, since he had a schedule to maintain. The bicyclist paid the fare for the melon, jumped on his bike, and sped off on a shortcut route.

By this time the interest of the weary homeward-bound bus passengers was aroused. Losing sight of the bicyclist for about two miles, they started speculating about his progress. When the bus approached the point where the two routes converged, they craned their necks and shouted, "Here he comes!" He was pumping hard and looked hot and tired, but he arrived at the intersection in time to receive his well-traveled watermelon, to the cheers of the passengers.

—Josephine Zwickl *(South Bend., Ind.)*

A WOMAN I know put this ad in the local paper: "Lost 50 pounds! Selling my fat clothes—good condition, sizes 18–20."

She was bombarded with phone calls, but nobody wanted to buy the clothes—they all wanted to know how she had lost the 50 pounds.

—Peggy Greco *(Irving, Texas)*

ON THE outskirts of a small town out West, we saw a sign reading: SLOW DOWN—SPEED 25 M.P.H. RIGIDLY ENFORCED.

I must have been slow to react because within a block we hit a deep, bone-shattering gap in the pavement, which left us wondering whether the car or the passengers would fall apart first. A few feet beyond was another sign, bearing just one word: SEE?

—Clarence D. Stallman *(Joliet, Ill.)*

WHEN an English business associate was visiting in our home one Thanksgiving, our young son asked him whether the English celebrated Thanksgiving. "Oh, yes, indeed," replied our friend. "But we celebrate it on the Fourth of July!"

—Donald W. Davis *(Milwaukee, Wis.)*

WHILE visiting a friend, I noticed that her four-year-old daughter frequently interrupted her housework by coming in and insisting that her mother "come outside and see." She would then excitedly show her mother a flower, a butterfly, a broken bird's egg or a crawling ant. After this had happened for about the sixth time, I remarked that these little trips certainly interfered with my friend's daily routine.

"Well," she replied cheerfully, "I brought her into the world. The least I can do is let her show it to me."

—Mrs. R. T. Eveland *(Levittown, Pa.)*

As I opened what looked like a wedding invitation or announcement, complete with inner envelope, I wondered for whom I would be buying a wedding gift now. But to my surprise the formal engraved announcement read:

> Frances K. Fischer
> is pleased to announce
> the loss of one hundred pounds
> by
> B. D. Fischer
> September 7, 1971—February 20, 1972

—A. Fischer *(Los Angeles, Calif.)*

"You Could Look It Up"

By JAMES THURBER

IT ALL BEGAN when we went down to C'lumbus, Ohio, from
Pittsburgh to play an exhibition game on our way out to St.
Louis. It was gettin' on into the season and though we'd been
leadin' the league by six, seven games, we was now only a
half a game ahead of St. Louis. Our slump had given the boys
the leapin' jumps. They was snarlin' at each other, eatin' bad
and sleepin' worse, and battin' for a team average of maybe
.186.

This was 50, 51 year ago, you could look it up. Squawks
Magrew was managin' the boys at the time, and he was darn
near crazy. He yelled at everybody and wouldn't listen to nobody without maybe it was me. I'd been trainin' the boys for
ten year.

Well, we lose two to Pittsburgh, so we snarled all the way
to C'lumbus, where we put up at the Chittaden Hotel. Everybody was tetchy, and when Billy Klinger took a sock at Whitey
Cott at breakfast, Whitey throwed marmalade in his face.

"Blind each other, whatta I care?" says Magrew. "You can't
see nothin' anyways."

C'lumbus win the exhibition game, 3 to 2, whilst Magrew
set in the dugout, mutterin' and cursin'. I told him he was
drivin' the boys crazy the way he was goin' on, sulkin' and
whinin'. I was older'n he was and smarter'n he was, and he
knowed it. I was ten times smarter'n he was about this Pearl
du Monville, first time I ever laid eyes on the little guy.

Now, most people name of Pearl is girls, but this Pearl du
Monville was a man, if you could call a fella a man who was

only 34, 35 inches high. Pearl du Monville was a midget. I can see him now, swingin' a bamboo cane and smokin' a big cigar. He talked like he was talkin' into a tin can. After the game with C'lumbus, Magrew headed straight for the Chittaden bar—the train for St. Louis wasn't goin' for three, four hours—and there he sat, drinkin' rye and talkin' to this bartender. He was settin' there, tellin' this bartender how heartbreakin' it was to be manager of a buncha blindfolded circus clowns, when up pops this Pearl du Monville outa nowheres, clumb up on a chair and says, "I seen that game today, Junior, and you ain't got no ball club. What you got there is a side show." Pearl du Monville stood up on his chair and waved his cane around and pretended like he was ballyhooin' for a circus. "Right this way, folks!" he yells. "Come on in and see the greatest collection of clowns in the world! See the pitchers who can't pitch, see the batters who can't hit, see the infielders with five thumbs!" and on and on like that, feedin' Magrew gall and handin' him a laugh at the same time, you might say.

You could hear him and Pearl du Monville hootin' and hollerin' way up to the fourth floor of the Chittaden and when it come time to go to the station the fellas left me to handle Magrew and his new-found crony. Well, I got 'em outta there finely. I had to take the little guy along, 'cause Magrew had a holt onto him like a vise. "He's comin' as masket," says Magrew. An' come along he did.

Well, sir, the first game with St. Louis was rained out, and there we was facin' a double-header next day. We lose the first game, 7 to 2, and the nightcap, 9 to 3, and that puts us into second place plenty, and as low in our mind as a club can get.

The next day was a horrible day, like anybody that lived through it can tell you. Practice was just over and the St. Louis club was takin' the field, when I hears this strange sound from the stands—it was the fans ketchin' sight of Pearl du Monville all dressed up in a minacher club uniform, sox, cap and all. He was out on the field swingin' a kid's bat and smokin' a cigar.

I went over to Magrew. "Is that any way to treat the uniform," I says, "makin' a mockery out of it?"

"It might surprise you to know I ain't makin' no mockery outa the uniform," says Magrew. "I got lawyer's papers on me," he says, "made out legal and proper, constitutin' one

Pearl du Monville a bone-of-fida member of this former ball club."

Well, sir, it'll all be there in the papers of 50, 51 year ago, and you could look it up. The game went along without no scorin' for seven innings. The fans pay most of their attention to Pearl du Monville out there in fronta the dugout, turnin' handsprings, balancin' his bat on his chin, walkin' an imaginary line.

So it went up to the lasta the eight, nothin' to nothin'. Our pitcher gets the first two men out easy. Then up come a fella name of Potter or Billings, and he lammed one up against the tobacco sign for three bases. The next guy up gets a hit, and in come the fella from third for the only run of the ball game. The looka death come onto Magrew's face.

Their next man fouled out backa third, and we come up for our last bats like a bunch of schoolgirls steppin' into a pool of cold water. When Gordy Mills hit out to second, I just closed my eyes. I opened 'em up again to see Dutch Muller standin' on second, dustin' off his pants, him havin' got his first hit in maybe 20 times to the plate. Next, Harry Loesing got a base on balls. Whitey Cott popped out to short. That brung up Billy Klinger, with two down and a man on first and second. Billy waits 'em out, and finely he walks, too, fillin' the bases.

Yes, sir, there you are; the tyin' run on third and the winnin' run on second, firsta the ninth, two men down, and Hank Metters comin' to bat. Hank couldn't run no faster'n President Taft, but he was hittin' better'n anybody else on the club.

"Wait a minute!" yells Magrew, jumpin' to his feet. "I'm sendin' in a pinch hitter!" he yells. "Du Monville battin' for Metters!"

I don't need to tell you Bethlehem broke loose on that there ball field! The fans got onto their hind legs, yellin' and whistlin' and hollerin'. When Pearl got up to the plate and stood there, the pitcher slammed his glove down onto the ground and started stompin' on it, and they ain't nobody can blame him—he's just walked two normal-sized human bein's, and now here's a guy up they ain't more'n 20 inches between his knees and his shoulders.

Then the plate umpire come over to Magrew and he told him to get a batter up, or he'd forfeit the game to St. Louis. Magrew pulls some papers outa his pocket and shows 'em to the umpire. And all this time the St. Louis manager and the fans and the players is yellin' and hollerin'.

Well, sir, they fought about him bein' a midget and they was eight or nine rule books brung out and everybody was thumbin' through 'em, trying to find out what it says about midgets, but it don't say nothin' about midgets, 'cause this was somethin' never'd come up in the history of the game before.

The plate umpire finely decided the contrack papers was all legal and he bawls, "Play ball!" The St. Louis pitcher picked up his glove, slams in the first pitch, hard and wild, and maybe two feet higher'n the midget's head.

"Ball one!" hollers the umpire over'n' above the racket.

The ketcher goes on out towards the mound, talks to the pitcher and hands him the ball. This time it comes in a little closer, maybe no higher'n a foot above Pearl's head.

"Ball two!" the umpire bellers.

The ketcher walks on out to the mound again, and the whole infield comes over and gives advice to the pitcher about what they'd do with two balls and no strikes on a batter that oughta be in a bottle of alcohol 'stead of in a big-league game between the teams that is fightin' for first place.

For the third pitch, the pitcher stands there flat-footed and tosses up the ball like he's playin' ketch with a little girl. Pearl stands there motionless as a hitchin' post, and the ball comes in big and slow and high—high for Pearl, that is, it bein' about on a level with his eyes, or a little higher'n a grown man's knees.

They ain't nothin' else for the umpire to do, so he calls, "Ball three!"

Everybody is onto their feet yellin' as the pitcher sets to throw ball four. It come in big as a balloon and slower'n any ball ever throwed before in the major leagues. It come right in over the plate in front of Pearl's chest, lookin' prob'ly big as a full moon to Pearl.

They ain't never been a minute like the minute that followed since the United States was founded by the Pilgrim grandfathers. Pearl du Monville took a cut at that ball, and he hit it!

Magrew give a groan like a pole-axed steer as the ball rolls out in fronta the plate and the midget starts runnin' for first, still carryin' that little bat, and makin' maybe 90 foot an hour. Bethlehem breaks loose. The ball's rollin' slow, on down towards third, goin' maybe eight, ten foot. The infield comes in fast and our boys break from their bases like hares in a brush fire.

The ketcher gets to the ball first, but he boots it on out past the pitcher's box, the pitcher fallin' on his face tryin' to stop it, the shortstop sprawlin' after it full length and zaggin' it on over towards the second baseman, whilst Muller is scorin' with the tyin' run and Loesing is roundin' third with the winnin' run. But Pearl is still maybe 15, 20 feet from the bag, toddlin' like a baby and yeepin' like a trapped rabbit. The second baseman finely gets aholt of that ball and slams it over to first. The base umpire waves Pearl out and there goes your old ball game, the craziest ball game ever played in the history of the organized world!

And then I see Magrew. He starts runnin' after Pearl. Pearl sees him comin' and runs behind the base umpire's legs. Magrew comes up, pantin' and roarin', and him and the midget plays ring-around-a-rosy with the umpire, who keeps shovin' at Magrew with one hand and tryin' to slap the midget loose from his legs with the other.

Finely Magrew ketches the midget. He gets hold of that little guy by both his ankles and starts whirlin' him round and round his head like Magrew was a hammer thrower and Pearl was the hammer. Then Magrew lets the midget fly. He flies on out towards second, high and fast, like a human home run, headed for the soap sign in center field and he's goin' to bust to pieces like a dollar watch on asphalt when he hits the ground. But it happens their center fielder is just crossin' second, and he starts runnin' back, tryin' to get under the midget. He goes back and back and he pulls that midget down outa the air like he was liftin' a sleepin' baby from a cradle. They wasn't a bruise onto him, only his face was the color of cat's meat.

Bethlehem was ragin' like Niagry on that ball field with the fans swarmin' onto the field, and the cops tryin' to keep order, and six or eight of us holdin' onto Magrew to keep him from gettin' at that midget.

I seen Pearl du Monville strugglin' in the arms of a lady fan with an ample bosom, who was laughin' and cryin' at the same time, and him beatin' at her with his little fists. He clawed his way loose finely and disappeared among everybody's legs. That was the last I ever seen of Pearl du Monville, and neither did nobody else.

That night we piled onto a train for Chicago, but we wasn't snarlin' and snappin' anymore. No, sir, the ice was finely broke with the disappearance of Pearl du Monville out backa second base. We got to laughin' and talkin' and kiddin' together, and 'fore long Magrew was laughin' with us. He got a human look onto his pan again, and he quit whinin' and complainin'.

Well, sir, we wiped up that Chicago series, winnin' all four games, and makin' 17 hits in one of 'em. We hit our home lot like a ton of dynamite and they was nothin' could stop us from then on.

I don't recollect things as clear as I did so I can't tell you the exact margin we win the pennant by. Maybe it was two and a half games, or maybe it was three and a half. But it'll all be there in the newspapers and record books of 50, 51 years ago. Like I say, you could look it up.

PERCENTAGE POINTS

AN ELECTED official is one who gets 51 percent of the vote cast by 40 percent of the 60 percent of voters who registered.
—Dan Bennett

AT A sidewalk clothing sale, a colorful poncho bore a tag which read: "Fibers 90 Percent Unknown, 10 Percent Other."
—Contributed by Mrs. Les Paulsen

THE AMERICAN shopper is that strange creature who will rush to a 10-percent-off sale and then let the carrying charges ride at 18 percent.
—Bill Copeland in Sarasota, Fla., *Journal*

DURING a heavy snowstorm in Grand Forks, N.D., radio announcer Orlie Knutson read this official forecast: "Ten-percent chance of precipitation. The low tonight will be 24 to 32 degrees." Then he added his *own* report: "The temperature is now 20 degrees, and it has been 10-percenting all afternoon."

FORTY PERCENT of American families own dogs, and—vice versa.
—Franklin P. Jones in *Quote Magazine*

Toward More Picturesque Speech II

Enjoying the Signery

In the window of a skin-diving-equipment store: "We carry a complete line of under ware"

(D. Deutsch)

At a golf driving range: "Hitch your braggin' to a par"

(B. Hopfensperger)

Spell-Binding

Anyone who has ever dealt with city, state and federal agencies spells it bureaucrazy

—Orben's Comedy Fillers

Do you ever get the feeling that life is a spelling bee and you've just been given SUPERCALIFRAGILISTICEXPIALIDOCIOUS?

—Orben's Comedy Fillers

Retort Time

To waiter: "Who prepared this Caesar salad? Brutus?"

—Anne Carroll

A Small Town Is . . .

where you squeeze a girl and everybody squeals
—Franklin P. Jones in *Quote Magazine*

where two's company and three's a demonstration
—*Orben's Current Comedy*

Autumn Moment

> *Something told the wild geese*
> *It was time to go.*
> *Though the fields lay golden*
> *Something whispered, "Snow."*

(Rachel Field)

BANNER BONERS

THE Halifax, Canada, *Herald* reported: "JUNE BABIES FLOOD OTTAWA HOSPITAL."

THE Spokane *Chronicle* announces: "GRILL SUSPECT OVER BIG BLAZE."

HEADLINE in Springfield, Mo., *Leader-Press:* "NEW ORLEANS POLICE WARM STRIP-TEASERS."

FROM the Springfield, Mass., *Union:* ESCAPED LEOPARD BELIEVED SPOTTED.

FROM the Middletown, Pa., *Journal:* OFFICERS' WIVES TO SELECT NEW OFFICERS.

FROM the Chicago *Southwest News-Herald:* FLORIST ASKS GIRLS TO DROP STRAPLESS GOWNS.

Good Clean Fun
in Finland

●‖●‖●‖●‖●‖●‖●‖●‖●‖●‖●‖●‖●‖●‖●‖●‖●‖●‖●‖●

By RED SMITH

●‖●‖●‖●‖●‖●‖●‖●‖●‖●‖●‖●‖●‖●‖●‖●‖●‖●‖●‖●

THE SAUNA is a Finnish bath, and a great deal more. It is a sacred rite, a form of human sacrifice in which the victim is boiled like a missionary, then baked to a turn, then beaten with sticks until he flees into the icy sea, then lathered and honed and kneaded and pummeled by the high priestess of this purgatorial pit.

Nothing relaxes a Finn like this ritual of fire worship, water worship and soap worship. It is an ancient folk custom dating from forgotten times, and it explains why Finland produces so many great marathon runners. Anybody who can survive a sauna can run 26 miles barefoot over broken beer bottles.

The most gracious gesture of hospitality a Finn can make is to bathe with his guest. From an American host, a suggestion that everybody go get washed might imply that the guest was a trifle gamy, but Americans don't know everything. "A foreigner," says a pamphlet on the subject, "who leaves Finland without the intimate acquaintance of a sauna cannot boast of having come to grips with the Finnish mentality. Through it the creature of civilization is enabled to get in touch with the primal forces of nature—earth, fire and water."

Curious about primal forces, three Americans and Kai Koskimies, their Finnish host, taxied out to Vaskiniemi, on the outskirts of Helsinki, where a birch forest meets the blue waters of the Gulf of Finland. There we entered a sauna, stripped to the buff and bowed cordially to the Lady of the Bath, an old doll wearing spectacles and a long rubber apron, busy soaping and scrubbing the tract of masculine meat on her pine-board table.

Then we entered the smoke room, a murky, low-ceilinged cubicle recognizable by anybody who ever read Dante. Several other lost souls attired in sweat sat on benches, faces buried in their hands. The room was heated—an understatement, as ever was—by a sort of Dutch oven in which cobblestones are cooked over a fire of birch logs. A thermometer registered only 130° Fahrenheit, and Kai, making a snoot of disapproval, scooped water onto the hot rocks to get up a head of steam.

The smoke room is the simple, ancient type of sauna, part of the humblest Finnish home. There are 900,000 of them in Finland, one for every six people. "The air gives off a slight but exhilarating aroma of smoke," says the pamphlet. "The effect of the open fireplace feels strong to sensitive people."

Three sensitive people stood it as long as any hickory-smoked ham could have done. Then we oozed out of the cell like melted tallow, and Kai led the way to another room, providing heat but without the smoke. There the thermometer outraged him. It registered only 176°, not even warm enough to boil an egg. The sauna proprietor agreed that this was ridiculous.

"This is no sauna," he said, and did something with the fireplace. "In one, two, three minutes it will be warm." In one, two, three minutes the thermometer raced up to 219. Missionaries are fricasseed at 212.

Bundles of leafy birch branches were provided as knouts so the bathers could beat themselves. Kai splashed water around to cool the wooden floor and benches, but it evaporated instantly. Even with the insulation of a folded Turkish towel, the seats were like stove lids.

Relaxing Finnish-style, everybody sat rocking from cheek to cheek to avoid being fried outright. At the same time, all laid about with the birch, flogging themselves like flagellants. After that came a refreshing dip in the sea.

The Gulf of Finland is colder than an Eskimo spinster. All feeling, however, had been left behind in the stewpot. The instant a guy hit the water he turned numb; he suffered no more than a corpse.

Cleanliness was next on the schedule, and the Lady of the Bath provided it. She starts with a shampoo, then works on the subject in sections—just as one eats a lobster, cleaning up one claw, laying it aside, and picking up another. Her powerful fingers probe deep, finding muscles the doctors have never charted. She is skillful, efficient and thorough. She scrapes the hull with a rough wet towel. The combination massage and scouring process is genuinely relaxing, easing muscles, untying knotted nerves.

That's all there is to a sauna, except for one technicality: as soon as you're finished, you do it all over—the heat and the swim. In the winter, when the sea drops two degrees in temperature and freezes over, you can't swim. You go outdoors and roll in the snow instead. On the second time around, the temperature in the dry oven had got satisfactorily cozy. It was slightly over 269° near the ceiling. This created some excitement around the sauna. They said it was a world record.

When it's all over, you get a diploma testifying that you are alive and clean. This is partly true.

MISSING INGREDIENTS

WHEN I had been married for nine years, I decided to return to work to augment the family income. I was pleased with how well our three children adjusted to the change, and at how efficiently I seemed to be managing as both housewife and secretary. Then one day I noticed that my small son was unusually quiet and thoughtful as he watched me rush about the kitchen preparing the evening meal. At last he said wistfully, "Mom, do you remember pies?"

—Contributed by Mary Linnell

Confessions of a
Dance-School Dropout

●❙●

By THOMAS BOLTON

●❙●

I KNEW I was in for it as soon as my wife Liz began to hum softly, swinging her honeyed hank of hair from pale shoulder to pale cheek. "Look," she said, "the Briscoes are dancing."

I took a steadying grip on my champagne glass. "Too crowded," I said. "Too hot. I don't know what that band's playing, but they're losing."

"The Thomases are dancing. So are the Disneys."

"Best way in the world to catch a cold. First you get over-heated, then the joints begin to stiffen and—"

"Are you going to ask me to dance?"

It did seem the politic thing to do. We were at an outdoor wedding reception. Acres of striped canvas had been pitched above a slick rink of wood. Four musicians, glum as owls, were perched nearby, playing a succession of relentlessly bouncy tunes.

On the dance floor Liz spun and we came together, snug as two spoons. "The best part about dancing," I said, "is that it's a contact sport."

"One, two, three. Now *try,"* she murmured.

"Okay," I said, and off we went, lurching in a generally clockwise direction. *Awful!* yelled the district attorney who lives in my head. *You were a dance-school dropout, you bombed at the senior prom and you are worse today.* Let a lovely girl press her fringe benefits against me, let the music begin—and I botch it all with my butter-fingered feet.

Suddenly I became aware that Liz had stopped dead in her

tracks. "Dear," she said, "do you recognize this tune?"

"How could I not?" I said cautiously. (Perhaps I had proposed to it.) "It's sort of our song, isn't it? *One* of our songs?"

"It's 'The Anniversary Waltz,'" she said, emitting an odd, high-pitched laugh. "You're doing the foxtrot. You are absolutely the worst dancer I've ever known."

"Honey," I soon said, "I'm going to make you an offer you can't refuse. Let's sit this one out."

"Done," she replied quickly. "You go first—I want to keep an eye on your feet."

Well, I was pretty sure that would be the end of it. I thought I knew what had made her so touchy. When you go to a wedding with your wife, you shouldn't keep referring to the groom as "that poor devil."

IT TURNED out that it wasn't the end. I got home from work the next Monday to find Liz humming cheerily in the kitchen. "Hi," I said. "You look like the proverbial cat who has supped on prime canary."

"I'm happy," she announced, "because I went and did it: I signed us up."

"You signed us up?" In my experience, very little good has ever come from those words.

"Darling, you know the Crestwood Adult School? I signed us up for their night course in social dancing!"

I gazed for a long moment out the window, toward the woods where the birds flew free.

"You'll love it!" Liz went on. "Remember how you used to practically *beg* me to dance when we were first dating? If you hate dancing so much, how do you explain that?"

"Lust. It was the quickest way to get my arms around you in a fashion acceptable to community standards. But, sweetheart, at the age of 38 a man learns to look his limitations squarely in the eye. I'll never climb Annapurna, or jump in the Plaza fountain at midnight. And I'll never, ever, be a social dancer."

"You *can* be," she whispered. "For us. For me."

When you play against Liz, you play against a stacked deck.

Social dancing was taught Thursday evenings in the school gymnasium, an enclosure musky with the scent of decades of adolescent endeavor. As we entered, a sense of doom overcame

me. The other couples there had this *nimble* look about them—
they stood flexing their knees, and in general seemed poised
to plunge into "Swan Lake."

Clapping his hands for attention, our instructor, Mr. Her-
nando Lopez, strode briskly forward. He was short and wide,
wore a shimmery maroon suit, and sported a small mustache
above a dazzling complement of teeth. "Welcome, dance ap-
prentices!" he shouted joyously. "Tonight we start with the
basics. One must learn to crawl before he walk, eh?" Mrs.
Lopez, large and resolute, dropped a record on the phonograph,
and husband and wife began dipping and heaving in a flurry
of Latin arabesques.

"You see?" demanded Lopez, his patent-leather pumps
flashing. "You see the grace, the feeling?" He twirled, pistol-
clapped his hands and looked at us with rapture. "You learn
to do cha-cha," he shot at us, "you can do *any* dance. She is
Rosetta Stone of social dancing!"

As we students began to dance, Lopez and wife prowled
among us, alert to any misstep or botched beat. If a woman
was spotted in a *faux pas,* Lopez would commandeer her and
demonstrate correct procedure; a bungling male would in turn
fall into the formidable clutches of Mrs. Lopez. Somehow I
managed to heave myself through a passable cha-cha each time
they strolled near. But when the hour was done, I was ex-
hausted—my heart leaping in my breast like a berserk maraca.
I had avoided the heavyweight embrace of Mrs. Lopez.

But at terrible cost. As we left, Liz said happily, "Darling,
you did *wonderfully!* You're really picking it up. I can hardly
wait till next week."

Next week! Suddenly the calendar seemed to stretch in front
of me like an endless dance card, upon which I was remorse-
lessly inked in as the beau of the ball.

No sooner had the pain in my calf muscles subsided than
next week was upon us, and there we were back on the basketball floor, going one-on-one. Only this time there was a
striking difference. Mrs. Lopez, her husband announced, had
hurt her ankle. In her place now stood a cousin, a spectacularly
fetching creature with prosciutto skin and dark coffee eyes.
The neckline of her gown came nowhere near her neck.

"Well," humphed Liz, eyeing the girl's assorted amplitudes,
"how obvious can you get?"

In other circumstances, I might have admired the girl with the enthusiasm that was her due. But at that point my basic interest was survival; there's no time for ogling on the tilting decks of a *Titanic*.

Lopez called muster and gave us a short pep talk. Then the record dropped like a guillotine and we resumed our ballroom labors. Suddenly Lopez detonated his palms and stabbed me with his forefinger. "Wrong!" he cried. "Carmen, you show him."

Before I quite knew what was happening, Carmen had insinuated herself into my arms, and warm Latin blood fairly hummed beneath my fingers. "You must surrender," she instructed. "Surrender to the music. *Feel* the rhythm. Your hand on my waist, like so."

She continued to talk away at me, but to no avail. The more she told me, the more numbly inept I became. Finally she recycled me back to Liz. "You learn," she said hopefully. "You practice."

I stumbled on. The trouble was, I just couldn't regain that fine edge of panic which, the week before, had hoisted me to the level of adequacy. I couldn't seem to synchronize hips and feet and breathing. Once I even stepped on my *own* toes. And of course by this time the indefatigable Carmen was tailgating me wherever I went, ready to whisk me like a broom across the floor. To her, I must have represented some sort of ultimate challenge.

In 1955, one Carlos Sandrini in Buenos Aires established the individual world record for continuous ballroom dancing: 106 hours, 5 minutes, 10 seconds. By nine that night, when the music was stilled at last, I felt that I had broken the record. "Thank God that's over," I said as I walked dazedly out with Liz. "Until next time, that is."

"Next time," she said. "What makes you think there'll be a next time?" The voice, usually so warm, was newly air-conditioned.

"Aren't there six more lessons? Barring a reprieve from the governor, of course."

"Please don't pretend you had a bad time. Let's at least be open with each other. Admit you loved every minute of it. You and that . . . that hot tamale!"

I walked on in momentary silence. The truth, of course,

was that I would as soon foxtrot with Larry Csonka as again come to grips with Carmen. But would truth, usually so admirable a standard, in this case best serve mankind? Put another way, would it get me anything more than six additional weeks of cha-cha lessons?

"Ah, Carmen," I murmured, feeling my way carefully. "Well, she does make it all come alive. A natural teacher with so much to give. Call it animal instinct."

"I knew it."

"Great eyes—and what a rhythm section!"

"That does it. We have just been to our last dance lesson."

"If you insist," I said, smiling into the darkness. I'd make it up to Liz, that very night: we'd stay up together and watch Fred Astaire on the "Late Show."

EXPLANATION POINTS

A SAN FRANCISCO bank cashier cashed six phony checks for the same forger within a two-week period. When police and the bank's manager asked the girl why she suspected nothing and kept cashing the checks, she explained, "Because he looked familiar."

—Contributed by Douglas Scott

REFUSING a cocktail at a dinner party, a young mother explained, "I don't believe in drinking in front of the children, and when they aren't around, who needs it?"

—Contributed by Mrs. Dale R. Ensinger

BALTIMORE *Sunday Sun* columnist Ralph Reppert says, "I cannot indulge in such sports as water skiing, mountain climbing and water polo because of my poor back—it has a big yellow streak running up it."

Hot Off the Gridiron

"Okay, Schultz, get in there now and block the referee's view!"

PORGES IN *SATURDAY REVIEW*

"I just love it! I always pretend it's ME they're after!"
FRANKLIN FOLGER, PUBLISHERS-HALL SYNDICATE

"What was confusing about it? The quarterback thought they'd red-dog him, so he called an automatic, bootlegged the ball, and then tossed a pass over the cornerback to his split end, who was on a zig-out pass pattern."
LEPPER IN *THE CHRISTIAN SCIENCE MONITOR*

"You, with all the advice—go in for Oblonsky!"
J. MIRACHI IN *THE SATURDAY EVENING POST*

"I DID leave him once, but he never noticed"
BETTY SWORDS, CARTOONS-OF-THE-MONTH

New Year's Day in the 1880's

●❙●❘●❙●❘●❙●❘●❙●❘●❙●❘●❙●❘●❙●❘●❙●❘●❙●❘●❙●❘●❙●❘●❙●

By SAMUEL HOPKINS ADAMS

●❙●❘●❙●❘●❙●❘●❙●❘●❙●❘●❙●❘●❙●❘●❙●❘●❙●❘●❙●❘●❙●❘●❙●

"HAPPY New Year's," said my two young cousins in unhappy voices. They were apprehensive of the unknown rites before us.

The fine flower of local custom in Rochester, N. Y., in the 1880's was New Year's hospitality. On that day the Old Families kept open house with pomp, circumstance and a lavish prodigality of refreshment equaled today only by a gangster's wake. This was pre-eminently a masculine day. The ladies stayed at home, cast in the role of providers, while young men and old made the rounds from high noon to 6 P.M., eating their voracious way like a swarm of social locusts.

For us small boys the round of calls was a kind of debut, often the first public tryout of manners formed at Miss Quinby's dancing class. It was thus something of an ordeal, the rigors of which were mitigated only by the prospect of the richest cuisine of the year. We knew, for instance, that the Brewsters would serve five kinds of pie; that the Rogers' chicken salad was beyond all competition; that the Stedmans could be relied upon for that rarest of luxuries, scalloped oysters; and that what was known as charlotte "roosh" attained its apex of delicacy at Miss Ada Kent's.

I was equipped with all this gastronomic information on the day of my debut, in 1881. My cousins, John and Sireno Adams, had joined me for the afternoon, and we were now lined up for scrutiny by our elders. All of us were in our best clothes, John in dark blue with brass buttons, Reno in fuzzy brown and new tight shoes, and I in my hitherto unworn pepper-and-salt

141

Norfolk suit. Grandfather was pleased to express his approval: "You look very macaroni."

Grandma repeated our instructions. Don't track snow into the house. Be sure to greet the hostess before eating and to say good-by before leaving. Take off gloves before shaking hands. Bow as Miss Quinby taught. Don't start tag-you're-it or any other game indoors. Don't ask for a second helping. Act like little gentlemen everywhere.

It was a large and depressing order.

Grandfather unexpectedly lightened our gloom when he announced that he would come with us and act as our coachman for the occasion. We piled into the sidebar cutter with whoops of joy, and off we went behind the venerable Adams nag, Horace G. (for Greeley). John ventured the suggestion that Grandfather give us his moral support by accompanying us into the first house.

"No, no," he said. "You must stand upon your own feet."

"Mine hurt," Reno said. "I wanta go home."

He was squelched and we were discharged on the corner of Plymouth Avenue. Each struggling to be last, we went into the Chamberlins' house. It was not nearly as bad as we had foreboded. Through this and the next few calls we bumbled without open disgrace. Presently our shyness evaporated in the simple warmth of the day's greetings. By an imperceptible transition, we became polished men of the world. John's comments on the weather were models of ease and felicity. I achieved a dexterity with gloves and handkerchief that would have done credit to Beau Brummell.

The first setback came as we approached the John Rochester mansion, famous for the richness of its refections. No festoons ornamented its front windows. The walk had not been cleared of snow. Halfway up the steps we were met by Boardman Smith, descending. He addressed us with the superciliousness proper to his 16 years. "N.G., kids; no grub. Basket."

"What's basket?" we asked, gaping.

"A basket hung to the door means the family's away and you can put your card in it and come back next year," Mr. Smith said scornfully.

That block was distressingly prolific of baskets, and we dispensed most of our elegant handwritten pasteboards. We did well at Livingston Park, though, and presently we had put in a solid foundation of edibles. It was time to crown it with the glorious superstructure of Miss Ada Kent's charlotte russe.

Miss Ada's reputation as a benefactor of youth was wide. She was a brisk little cricket of 25, a predestined old maid. Her table at Sunday-school picnics was always the most lavish. With the first sufficient snowfall she took a chosen few on a bobsleigh hayride. Her popularity was second only to that of Santa Claus.

Some other boys of our crowd were skylarking in front of the Kent gate when we drove up. Our arrival roused them to good-natured violence, and, in the free-for-all that ensued, John lost three highly essential buttons from the front of his short pants. It could not have happened to a more modest boy. He was for withdrawing to the shelter of the cutter while the rest of us enjoyed the ambrosia of the Kent setout.

Grandfather vetoed this. A conference was held. Jumbo Emerson contributed a scarfpin to the cause of respectability, repairs were made, John was cautioned to move gingerly and we all trooped up the steps.

Miss Ada's pleasure at our advent was heartwarming. "Dear boys," she beamed, "I do hope you have brought your appetites with you."

The main parlor and sitting room were full of grownups, but in the side parlor a special trestle had been reserved for youth. In the center of the snowy damask tablecloth towered a massive charlotte russe. Several little girls, starched, sashed and beribboned, were deputed to wait upon us. We seated ourselves on opposite sides of the makeshift table.

All might have gone well had not John overextended himself in reaching for a plate of ladyfingers. Something slipped. An expression of acute anguish froze his face. His hands fumbled in his lap. Plainly he was making private and desperate adjustments. I noticed the tablecloth twitch slightly, but did not interpret the movement until too late.

Vern Fitzsimmons also had observed John's maneuvers. Vern was precociously quick-witted and tactful. He craned his neck to look out the window. "Say, John," he exclaimed, "your horse is getting fidgety. Better get out there."

"Thanks, Vern," John said gratefully. He rose and started for the door—and the tablecloth moved with him. The serried array of knives, forks and spoons broke ranks and cascaded to the floor. Two candy bowls rolled merrily after and, in final catastrophe, the lofty charlotte russe toppled onto Miss Ada's carpet. All the little girls shrieked in chorus. Miss Ada did a maidenly faint.

Grandfather, dozing in the cutter, was wakened by Horace G. giving a mighty start against the dashboard. The old horse had reason to be shocked. John, the mild-mannered, the paragone of correct behavior, was stumbling and staggering down the steps, clutching himself amidships, trailing interminable lengths of white damask. After him swarmed a turbulent crowd of his fellows, hysterical with mirth, shouting the refrain of a popular song made for such occasions:

Whoa, Emma! Whoa, Emma!

Emma, you put me in such a dilemma!

Grandfather scrambled nimbly from beneath his lap robe. "Get in, John," he said in a tone of quiet command. The old gentleman detached Miss Ada's best napery, lifted the squirming boy into the cutter, and with a sharp "Gid-*app*, Horace," drove away, leaving Reno and me to walk home.

A year later, on January 1, 1882, a basket dangled inhospitably from Miss Ada Kent's doorknob. It may have been the aftermath of John's mischance. Or it may have been a *non sequitur*. Nobody knows.

THE MONA LISA

I'LL NEVER understand how some people do the Louvre in one morning. I can't tell you how many mornings I have spent just in front of the Mona Lisa. Not that I'm such an art lover. I'm in love with the art lovers who show up in front of her. One morning I was standing in front of the Mona Lisa, and this man standing next to me said to his wife, "For this you drag me to Paris? We've got the same picture hanging in our bedroom." And his wife said, "And in a nicer frame."

—Selma Diamond

Humor in Uniform II

●||●||●||●||●||●||●||●||●||●||●||●||●||●||●||●||●||●||●||●||●||●||●||●||●||●

●||●||●||●||●||●||●||●||●||●||●||●||●||●||●||●||●||●||●||●||●||●||●||●||●||●

WHILE at Great Lakes Naval Training Station, a buddy and I in a restaurant eavesdropped as the sailor in the next booth was getting acquainted with his date. Everything seemed to be going well, until she suddenly said curtly, "All right, sailor—all hands on deck!"

—B. Bevill *(Westchester, Ill.)*

ON Navy Day, 1946, our submarine, the USS *Balao,* visited New York. All day long we escorted visitors through the boat, explaining the workings of various controls. Such routine work made us feel like beasts of burden.

Sitting at the evening meal, we were relaxing at being sailors again when suddenly a boy's head poked through the galley hatch and an excited voice exclaimed, "Hey, Mom! They're feedin' 'em!"

—Delbert Carper *(St. Paul, Minn.)*

GRAFFITI on ammo vests and helmets are usually at their wittiest among line troops, but none topped the one I read on the flak jacket of a clerk typist in Phu Bai, Vietnam. "Retreat, hell!" it said. "Back space."

—Cpl. C. O. Henderson, USMC *(FPO, San Francisco, Calif.)*

AT A SUNDAY service on an air base in Saudi Arabia, the chaplain announced: "This morning, I'm going to preach on the serviceman's misuse of the word 'hell.'" He then discussed the absurdity and poverty of expression betrayed by such phrases as: "What the hell do you want?" "Get the hell in here!" "Where the hell have you been?"

Standing at the door after the benediction, greeting the worshipers as they emerged, he received this compliment: "Chaplain, that was a helluva good sermon!"

—TSgt. Charles McKinney, Sr. *(Webb AFB, Texas)*

As a Navy wife, I long ago became accustomed to my husband's calling a floor a deck, a wall a bulkhead and our bathroom the head. I was not even greatly surprised to receive messages of "well done" after the birth of each of our children. But I was taken aback, the first night after a long sea-duty separation, when my husband looked over at me in bed and announced, "It's good to have you alongside."

—Jean P. Sundt *(Bonita, Calf.)*

An American aircraft carrier in the port of Genoa was expecting a visit by an important Italian naval officer, and prepared to render him full honors. Soon, a launch approached and a distinguished-looking man in uniform stepped smartly up the carrier's ladder. The band struck up the proper processional music for such prestigious occasions, and the welcoming ceremony went without a flaw. Later, the officers in charge of the carrier learned that they had piped aboard the city's chief garbage collector!

It was most embarrassing, but not without a happy ending. The garbage service the carrier received during the rest of its stay in Genoa was magnificent!

—Lt. Cdr. Thomas W. Schaff in *U.S. Naval Institute Proceedings*

During the war my father hitched a ride on a Navy plane. Snow, mixed with freezing rain, was coming down. "I hope you have good de-icing equipment," my father said to the pilot.

"Oh, yes," the pilot reassured him. "We have the very latest."

"Thank goodness!" said my father.

"Yes," the pilot continued, pointing to a pile of boxes in the back of the plane. "I'm on my way to a Naval air station in Rhode Island to have it installed."

—Louise S. Stone *(Bethesda, Md.)*

Our company in Vietnam had gathered to listen to our new C.O.'s welcoming speech. "I want you men to respect me as your leader, of course," he said. "But if you've got any problems, feel free to talk with me as if I were your father."

A voice boomed from the rear: "Hey, Pop, can I use the jeep tonight?"

—William Letourneau *(Lawrence, Mass.)*

IT WAS the last day of our basic training, and it was hard to believe that after breakfast we would be turned loose for a long-awaited 15-day leave.

We had a battalion-size mess hall, which meant that a man's position in line could be anywhere from 1 to 1000 and, as usual, our company had the honor of bringing up the rear. While we were waiting for the mess-hall doors to be opened, one soldier began at the end of the line saying good-by to each man and congratulating him for so patriotically and honorably suffering through basic and proving himself to be part of the cream of American manhood.

Most of us, charmed with his goodwill and warm handshake, smilingly watched him—until we suddenly realized that Mr. Happy's goodwill tour was leading him to the front of the line, so that when the doors were opened he was No. 1.

—T. H. Callahan *(Madison, Wis.)*

IT WAS Sunday evening, and the railroad station in Milwaukee was filled with sailors waiting for the train which would take them back to the Great Lakes Naval Training Center. Across the restaurant counter from me, four young sailors watched the attractive waitress with appreciative eyes. One asked, "Do you take orders to go out?"

"Sure," she said.

"Okay," he said with a grin. "Get your coat!"

—Mrs. Reid Hutchinson *(Hancock, Wis.)*

ONE of my jobs with the British army in Egypt was to organize concerts. This meant not only getting players and singers together but also finding someone to type out the programs.

On one occasion we had scheduled a violinist and pianist to play Handel's Sonata in A Major. The orderly-room clerk got the particulars right, but gave them an unusually military spacing:

Sonata in A . . . . . Major Handel

—Ian Parrott *(Aberystwyth, Wales)*

THE OFFICERS assigned to a military-assistance advisory group with the Chinese Republic military forces on Taiwan were searching for a name for their new officers' club. They finally agreed on: "TAI-WAN-ON."

—J. A. Ward, Jr. (Fayetteville, N.Y.)

IN AN insurance application, a chap giving information on his military background came to the question: "What did you do while in service?"

"AS TOLD!" he wrote in large letters.

—Carol Henry *(Birmingham, Ala.)*

OUR SON in the Marine Corps wanted to be an usher at his sister's wedding, so he went before his commanding officer and asked for leave. It was refused. "Sir," he protested, "I must be there. I'm the best man."

"But, corporal, you said you were an usher."

"Sir, my sister is marrying an Army man, two of the ushers are Navy, one is Air Force and I'm a Marine. So, sir, I repeat— I'm the best man!"

He got five days' leave.

—Mrs. Cecil Smith *(Arlington, Va.)*

ABOARD the carrier U.S.S. *Saratoga*, an officer walking through the mess deck noticed a cook with his feet propped up on a table. "Son," he asked, "do you put your feet on the furniture at home?"

"No, sir," replied the mess cook.

"Then why do you do it here?"

"Well, sir, at home airplanes don't land on the roof."

—Darrell E. Whitney, AO2, USN *(Lisbon Falls, Maine)*

I HAD just completed WAC basic training, and was traveling by train to see my sister on a five-day pass. Determined to uphold the honor of the corps, I tried valiantly to ignore the group of attractive Marine officers at the end of the car, who were obviously discussing me.

Finally, a young lieutenant approached and suggested that I have lunch with them. I was very cool, and when he eventually asked what was wrong, I reminded him primly that enlisted personnel are not permitted to fraternize with officers.

He returned to his group, and I heard him tell them, "She pulled rank on me!"

—Peggy Phillips *(Reno, Nev.)*

The Devious Art
of Place Dropping

●||●||●||●||●||●||●||●||●||●||●||●||●||●||●||●||●||●||●||●||●||●||●

By COREY FORD

●||●||●||●||●||●||●||●||●||●||●||●||●||●||●||●||●||●||●||●||●||●||●

THERE'S an indoor game that is bound to be very popular at social gatherings called Place Dropping. The object is to work into your table conversation (very casually; that's the whole game) the name of somewhere you've been. If nobody else has been there, it counts ten and you can talk without interruption through the rest of the dinner.

The trick is to sort of slip in the fact that you've been to a Place without coming right out and stating so. You never say to your dinner partner, "We went to Yurrop," for instance. Instead you glance at your watch and remark: "Well, right now it would be one o'clock back in Paris."

Or else you observe with a rueful shake of your head: "I just can't get used to these modern airplanes; this time yesterday we were having lunch in Wien—or, as you probably call it, Vienna." (Part of the game is to use a foreign name and then explain that München is really Munich, you know.)

There are various ways to maneuver into a good scoring position. One Place Dropper I know hits the basket every time by referring to his weight. "I bet I put on ten pounds this summer—that good old German *dunkles Bier.*"

Another Dropper shoots a consistently high score by bringing up the international date line. "I never can remember whether you gain a day or lose it; let's see, this would be Monday in Nippon. Japan, that is."

Water is usually a good opening—"I got the worst case of dysentery in Chile"—and food is always surefire. "Did you ever eat baby squid? We found the quaintest little restaurant in Athens. . . ." "I never thought I'd like fried seaweed, but in Hong Kong . . ."

As a rule, female Droppers prefer the underhand toss. "What a pretty tablecloth, dear; did you get it in Portugal? Oh, really?" with a condescending smile. "You ought to go to Lisbon sometime. They have the most beautiful linen."

On the other hand, male Droppers like to try a direct shot from the center of the floor. "Pretty good stuff, hah? Brought it back from Scotland myself."

Sometimes a successful Drop can be achieved without mentioning the Place at all. A skillful player just pulls a matchbox out of his pocket with "Air France" or "The Raffles Hotel, Singapore" on the cover, or absently hands the taxi driver a couple of drachmas or maybe an Indian rupee. A direct hit can be scored by simply carrying a tweed topcoat inside out so the Glasgow label shows.

Dropsmanship is a highly competitive sport. Topping another Dropper counts double, and the strategy is to steal the opponent's play. The other night at dinner the lady beside me said she simply adored Fraunts (Place Droppers are also Accent Droppers) and oh! to be back in la belle Paree, sipping a glass of shabley on the Shonz L S A.

The man on her right said that speaking of wine, they had a coconut drink in Ind-juh that would knock your hat off, and the lady beside him wondered if it was anything like the distilled cactus juice she had in May-heeco. A man sitting opposite said quickly that in Iceland he once drank fermented seal blubber, and the hostess inquired triumphantly whether anyone had ever tried Mongolian yak milk.

I didn't hear how the game came out, because I ducked around the corner for a glass of beer. The bartender said it wasn't like the stuff you get in Dublin, though.

JOB LOTS

As I look out of my office window, I can see a large billboard raised about 12 feet above the ground. One day I saw a new sign being installed, showing two bikini-clad girls reclining on the beach. When the workman finished passing the sign, he gathered up his tools. Before descending the ladder, he paused for a moment, reached over and lightly patted one of the girls on her suntanned derriere.

—Contributed by Ethel V. Mazer

An AUTOMOBILE serviceman specializing in foreign cars in a Minnesota town sent out a business card listing these mechanics:

Charles Nicholas ....for British autos
Karl Niklaus .... Volkswagen specialist
Carlos Niccoli ....for Italian models
Charles Nicolles ....for French cars
Carl Nikkoles .... for Swedish makes
    The serviceman who sent the card—Charlie Nicholas.

—Contributed by Carol B. Nestrud

Our SMALL manufacturing company supplied parts to the appliance industry, and one of our largest customers was notoriously slow to pay. When all standard collection pleas failed, I decided to try a humorous telegram to the company president. The results were amazing, and each month, after receipt of my buffoonery, the account was paid. But eventually I ran out of ideas for anything humorous or clever to say and dispatched a routine wire.

On my desk the next morning was the company president's succinct reply: NO FUNNY, NO MONEY.

—Contributed by S. D. Andrews

Living With Murder

By STEPHEN LEACOCK

I AM a great reader of detective fiction. But I see I shall have
to give it up. It begins to affect one's daily life too much. I
find myself perpetually "timing" myself. They always *time*
everything in the stories, so as to have it ready for the evidence.

For instance, I went to dine three or four days ago with my
old friend Jimmy Douglas. He lives alone. This, by itself,
would make any reader of crime fiction time him. I paused a
moment at the lighted doorway before ringing the bell and
noted that my watch said 7:00 P.M. A street clock, however,
marked 7:02½ P.M. I was thus able to place the time fairly
accurately as at 7:01¼.

I rang the bell, and a Chinese servant showed me noiselessly
into *apparently* empty sitting room. I say *apparently*, because
in the stories you never know. There might be a body lying
hunched up in a corner. There was an Ormolu clock on the
mantel (there always is) which I was checking over when Douglas came in.

I could only describe his manner as quiet. Certainly he was
free from any exhilaration. Whether this was a first effect of
arsenic poisoning, or just from seeing me, I am not prepared
to state. We had a cocktail. Douglas left two distinct fingerprints on his glass. I held mine by the rim. We sat down to
dinner at 7:30 P.M. Of this I am practically certain because I
remember that Douglas said, "Well, it's half-past," and as he
said it the Ormolu clock chimed the half-hour.

I noticed that at dinner Douglas took no soup. I took care
on my part to take no fish. This, in the event of arsenic poison,

would by elimination give indication of how the poison had been administered.

I got to talking and Douglas, I noticed, seemed after a while unable to listen without signs of drowsiness. This might be due to arsenic poisoning. I left at nine, having noticed that Douglas roused up with a slight start as the Ormolu clock struck, and said, "Nine! I thought it was ten."

I drove home in a taxi, and can easily identify the taxi, even if abandoned in a stone quarry, by a mark I made in the leather.

That was three days ago. I open the newspaper every morning with a nervous hand, looking for the finding of Douglas's body. They don't seem to have found it yet. I am all ready if they do. I have the taxi and the fingerprints and the Ormolu clock—that's all you need usually.

LOST CAUSE

ON THE morning following the college Winter Sports Festival, our American literature professor was giving a lecture on Emerson's famous essay "Self Reliance." "The civilized man has built a coach, but has lost the use of his feet," the professor quoted. "He is supported on crutches, but lacks so much support of muscle."

At this point the door opened and revealed a skiing victim of the sports festival—a lovely co-ed leaning on crutches, her foot in a large white cast. On either side of her stood a handsome young man. One of them carried her books. The other her purse and gloves and a single snow boot. They held the door open for her, helped her to a chair, took her coat and hung it up, and propped her crutches beside her.

When she was finally settled and the young men had departed, our professor spoke. "Your rebuttal is very effective, Miss Olson," he said. He stuffed his lecture notes into his pocket. "Class dismissed."

—Contributed by Mrs. Dennis Griffin

Corporate Images

LEO CULLUM IN *THE SATURDAY EVENING POST*

"Emily, I've just cleared my desk
and I'm taking the afternoon off."
HENRY MARTIN IN *SATURDAY REVIEW*

AL KAUFMAN IN *THE WALL STREET JOURNAL*

Plainfield's
Phantom Football Team

●II●II●II●II●II●II●II●II●II●II●II●II●II●II●II●II●II●II●II●II

By BOB COOKE

●II●II●II●II●II●II●II●II●II●II●II●II●II●II●II●II●II●II●II●II

WHO could forget that football season of 1941? Few of us hard-bitten sportswriters thought that the major post-season event would be a World War. No, we were after the big story, which usually revolved around the passing arm of Angelo Bertelli and the Notre Dame team that had juggernaut potential. There was also a pretty fair quarterback at Northwestern, a kid named Otto Graham. But, as we were to learn, the biggest football story of all was being written by a most unlikely author.

IT WAS a Friday morning in early September, and Morris New-burger, a partner in the Wall Street brokerage firm of New-burger, Loeb & Co., had just stretched himself in the big chair behind his office desk to read the sports page of the morning newspaper. "Damn! Damn! Damn!" cried Newburger, glancing at the headlines. "Oklahoma, Alabama, Michigan State! Never a word about the small colleges—not a line about the little teams!" Permit me to give you a brief sketch of Morris New-burger. As a child, he was clumsy, awkward and overweight. Throughout his school years his major contribution to athletics was as waterboy on his varsity football team.

Possibly it was this modest background that inspired New-burger to greater heights on that September Friday, as he sat there bitterly contemplating headlines that forever praised the skills of gridiron giants. Newburger switched the intercom button on his desk and told his secretary: "Please hold my calls."

His master plan was beginning to materialize. Newburger wrote down several fictitious college names and ultimately drew a circle around the plebeian-sounding "Plainfield Teachers," inspired by a suburban New Jersey town. He immediately realized he would need nine plausible opponents to make up a schedule, and it was at this point that he began to display his genius. In its completed form, the Plainfield Teachers 1941 football schedule looked like this:

Sept. 27—Plainfield vs. Benson Institute

Oct. 4—Plainfield vs. Scott

Oct. 11—Plainfield vs. Chesterton

Oct. 18—Plainfield vs. Fox

Oct. 25—Plainfield vs. Winona

Nov. 1—Plainfield vs. Randolph Tech (Away)

Nov. 8—Plainfield vs. Ingersoll (Traditional Rival)

Nov. 15—Plainfield vs. Appalachian Normal

Nov. 20—Plainfield vs. Harmony Teachers (Homecoming)

Impatiently Newburger awaited the afternoon of Saturday, September 27, 1941. Then at approximately five o'clock he dialed the New York *Herald Tribune*.

"Sports department, please," he said.

In a moment, a voice rasped "Sports!"

"I've got the Plainfield Teachers score," he said. "It's Plainfield Teachers 20, Benson Institute 0." The newsman thanked him and hung up. Newburger was in business.

He next telephoned the score to the Associated Press, the United Press, the New York *Times* and other news media. One can imagine his ecstasy the following morning when he opened the sports pages. Sure enough, there was the Plainfield Teachers score right along with the major college results.

Let it be said for Morris Newburger that he didn't take Sunday off. After all, he reasoned, you can't have a miracle team without a miracle player. So, he invented the celebrated Plainfield halfback, John Chung.

A big bruising runner who weighed 212 pounds, Chung was a "full-blooded Chinese" who gained an average of 7.9 yards every time he carried the ball, due largely, so Newburger said, to his habit of eating wild rice between the halves. On the following weekend, after Plainfield had defeated Scott, Newburger telephoned the result, and also filed a paragraph over the Western Union wire which reported that Chung had scored both Plainfield touchdowns.

Before Plainfield's third game against Chesterton, Newburger decided he needed a sports-information director. He invented a Jerry Croyden for the task, and New York sportswriters were duly impressed when they received Plainfield releases that came: "From the Desk of Jerry Croyden." (The name was picked out of the air while its creator was walking by Manhattan's Croydon Hotel.)

A sportswriter named Herb Allan, toiling for the New York *Post,* received a Croyden bulletin extolling Chung's wizardry and wrote a whole feature on the indestructible Chinese the following day. Croyden responded by advising the nation's press that the Plainfield team's colors were mauve and puce.

As the autumn weeks went by, Newburger created other Plainfield stars, one of whom was a six-foot-three pass receiver whom Newburger christened "Boarding House Smithers." Plainfield's coach was a tough but sage strategist known as "Ralph 'Hurry-Up' Hoblitzel."

It's a matter of record that Chung, Smithers and the other Plainfield heroes registered seven straight victories. Rival defenses all fell before Chung, who by then was being given monickers like "The Celestial Comet" by sportswriters who used Croyden-sent material.

The big game for New York sportswriters on October 25th was Fordham's 28–14 win over Texas Christian. But if you read the *Times* or the *Tribune* or the Philadelphia *Record* the next day, you would have also found Plainfield's 27–3 victory over Winona duly recorded. (Plainfield had posted shut-outs to that point; Newburger reluctantly let Winona have a field goal in the name of plausibility.)

On November 1, Notre Dame and Army played to a monumental 0–0 tie. But the Sunday-paper round-up also showed clearly that Plainfield had walloped Randolph Tech, 35–0. The following Saturday, as Harvard beat Army 20–6, John Chung led Plainfield to its seventh straight win, 13–0 over Ingersoll.

Newburger's enthusiasm knew no bounds. Croyden issued a full team roster that had a "Morris Newburger" at quarterback and named actual partners of Newburger, Loeb & Co. at key positions. But Newburger added plot as well as cast. In the game against Harmony Teachers, Chung was to be injured slightly and carried off the field, but not on any ordinary stretcher—the Chinese star would be carted to the sidelines by rickshaw.

Newburger also had a post-season game scheduled for Plainfield Teachers—a New Year's Eve contest called the Blackboard Bowl. Newburger had grown weary of the popular football formations such as the winged T and the double wing. So he had Coach Hoblitzel invent a brand-new formation which Jerry Croyden would outline in depth for members of the press. When the Plainfield players lined up with the ball in their possession, the two ends would face their own backfield. "In this way," Croyden explained in a release, "our ends can see immediately who has the ball."

AT THE desk next to mine in the New York *Herald Tribune's* sports department sat an alert reporter named Caswell Adams. I'll never forget the way he looked when he walked in one day in mid-November. Adams knew he had a big story and you could see his eagerness.

Adams admitted it was pure luck. He had a friend who had somehow gotten wind of Newburger's phone calls. (A phone had been installed for Jerry Croyden's personal use at Newburger's office.) The next day, Adams broke the story of the hoax in the *Herald Tribune*.

For Newburger it was a tragic day. His plans hadn't called for anything like this. Plainfield, with seven straight victories under its belt, was to have beaten Appalachian Normal. Then, in the finale, before a wildly enthusiastic homecoming crowd, Plainfield would subdue a gritty Harmony team, 40 to 27, on Thanksgiving Day, as Chung's exploits provided a clear margin of victory over Plainfield's "bigger opponents."

Before passing into oblivion, the stricken Jerry Croyden produced one more press release. "Midterm examinations proved a tougher hurdle for Plainfield's football team than any of its previous opponents," began Croyden's last opus. "Six of the 15 members of the football squad were declared ineligible today, and as a result Coach Ralph Hoblitzel has ordered the two remaining games canceled."

Chung was listed among those "thrown for a loss" by examinations. Morris Newburger went back to his stocks and bonds.

Both Newburger and Caswell Adams are gone now, eternal ticket-holders in the ultimate reserved-seat section. I became fascinated by Newburger's genius after I interviewed him to follow up the story. I admired Adams as well, and no sportswriter of the time can forget how he began his exposé:

Far above New Jersey's swamplands
Plainfield Teachers' spires
Mark a phantom, phony college
That got on the wires....

WORKING ARRANGEMENTS

I WENT to the railroad station one evening to get some information, but there was no one at the open ticket window. As I waited, a man came in and stood behind me. He seemed in a dreadful rush, standing first on one foot and then the other. Finally he shouted, "Why isn't anyone here to wait on us? With the fare we have to pay—it's disgraceful!"

Then he got really mad. "I'll just get what I want myself!" he yelled, and barged through the office door. Coming back to the window from the inside, he looked out at me and said, "What was it you wanted? I'll get it for you since I'm here."

Horrified, I stammered out, "I'm not really in that much of a hurry. I'll wait for the ticket agent."

"I am the ticket agent," he said. "I just wanted to see what it felt like to be on the other side for once."

—Contributed by Alice F. Grannon

THE PROCEDURE in our department is for each piece of correspondence to carry in the lower left-hand corner the director's initials in upper-case letters, followed by a colon and the typist's initials in lower case. One morning, the director suddenly summoned a new secretary into his cubicle for an animated conference. When she came out, carrying a sheet of paper, she told us with a smile, "Oh, he just asked me not to use my middle initial in the letters I type." Then she showed us the reason. In the lower left-hand corner was: GAS:bag.

—Contributed by Consuella P. Winder

Life in These United States® IV

●‖●

●‖●

IT WAS a Friday afternoon, and one of our friends gave little thought to having his power mower borrowed by a neighbor, until he happened to mention it to another neighbor. Then he discovered that this neighbor's mower had also been borrowed. Later, he was even more surprised to learn that three more mowers had been loaned to the same man.

When the hoarder was pressed for an explanation, he assured the men that all mowers would be returned bright and early Monday morning. "This is one weekend," he added with a grin, "that I intend to sleep late—in peace."

—Mary M. Kowalchik *(Galion, Ohio)*

AMERICANS, as I've discovered in my medical practice, seem unable to relax. A business executive came to my office for a routine checkup. He showed visible signs of overwork. I warned him to slow down, take up a hobby—perhaps painting—to relax. He readily agreed, and left the office.

The next day he phoned and announced enthusiastically, "Doc, this painting is wonderful! I've finished a dozen already."

—A. F. Johnson, M.D. *(Bremerton, Wash.)*

IN ORDER to save money on a trip to Hawaii, my sister and I had made our own wardrobes. Our first evening in the islands, I was ready for romance and adventure. Dressed in my most glamorous gown, I strolled down to the beach. The guitars were playing "Sweet Leilani," and the perfume of the tropical flowers was intoxicating. Soon I heard steps approaching from behind. "Pardon me," said a middle-aged woman with a south-western twang. "Isn't that Simplicity Pattern #6209?"

—Marjorie K. Pirtle *(Bainbridge Island, Wash.)*

LAST SPRING, my husband bought a 36-foot cabin crusier—his very first boat. He tried to talk like a seasoned yachtsman, with one salty term after another rolling glibly off his tongue, but in his heart "starboard" was still right, "port" left, and the "bow" and "stern" were still the front and back of the boat.

Sea language completely abandoned him the day we hit some submerged rocks. Not knowing that there normally is water in the bilge, he opened the forward hatch, saw it sloshing about and assumed that we were about to sink. As he grabbed the radio-telephone (which he kept tuned to the Coast Guard station "just in case"), his mind blanked on the international call for a ship in distress. "Maytag!" he shouted. "Maytag! Maytag!"

—Mrs. Albert F. Hockstader *(New Canaan, Conn.)*

AT THE TIME my daughter, Wendy, offered to take care of a friend's dog for a few days, her husband was working a night shift. It was a temporary assignment, and they were living in a trailer park. The dog, a large mixed breed named Fred, couldn't adjust his size and exuberance to the small trailer, and tried to escape each time the door was opened. Visiting Wendy one day, I found the dog tied firmly to a post outside. "What's with Fred?" I asked.

Wendy gave me a weary look. "That dog," she said, "has ruined my reputation. Last night, about nine o'clock, he got loose and took off through the park. I went after him shouting 'Fred, Fred, come back!' Everybody knows that my husband's name is Al," she sighed, "and that he works nights!"

—Alison W. Birch *(Kent, Conn.)*

IT WAS October, and New England had put on its pyrotechnic display of foliage. I was in Vermont spending a lazy afternoon sitting with a farmer on his stone wall beside the road. Several out-of-state cars sped past leaving jet streams of dust in their wake. When a car with a New York license hurtled by, my friend shook his head and commented, "Another city fellow out to see the country on his coffee break."

—Bob Brown *(Higganum, Conn.)*

OUR desert-reared children recently made their first visit to the Midwest. We hadn't realized just how narrow their geographical scope had been until one shouted excitedly, "Hey! They've got *water* under their bridges!"

—Mrs. R. J. Ream *(Phoenix, Ariz.)*

MY GOLFING partner and I were playing a roller-coaster-like course, which was covered with hundreds of white toadstools the size of golf balls. We had wasted many minutes walking from one white spot to another—finding our balls only by a process of elimination.

"I'll not lose another ball," announced my partner as he pulled from his bag a bright yellow ball. "Look at this jewel."

He teed up and hit a good drive down the middle. After I hit, we walked off the tee and out onto the crest of a hill from which we could see the area of the fairway where our balls would be. This time there were no white toadstools—only hundreds of bright yellow dandelions.

—Bill Gentry *(Union, W. Va.)*

WHEN we started planning a family camping trip, a friend advised my father to pack everything in beer cases instead of suitcases, because the beer cases would fit easily into the camper, were easy to move around, and could be marked to indicate their contents.

The first night, we were to stay at a fancy hotel in Chicago as a treat for my mother, who was somewhat dubious about the camping idea. Pulling up in front of the hotel, and seeing a bellboy approach, my father suddenly remembered that we had no luggage. Whereupon he opened the door of the camper and, pointing nonchalantly at the beer cases, said to the boy, "The Pabst, the Schlitz and the Budweiser go."

—Mrs. William M. Vaglienti, Jr. *(Wallingford, Conn.)*

JIM is a skilled home-handyman, and both he and his wife use the appropriate technical terms when speaking of his work. Recently, while he was resetting the tile in one of their bathrooms, a neighbor came to call. Jim joined his wife in chatting with her for a few minutes, then stole quietly back to his work. "Where's Jim?" asked the neighbor. "I didn't see him leave."

"Oh," replied Jim's wife, "he's gone to the bathroom to spackle and grout."

"Isn't it awful?" said the visitor with a shake of her head. "My husband had it all last week."

—A. V. Wyss *(Hopewell, Va.)*

THE CIGARETTE machine in our office often jams and, consequently, is physically assailed by its patrons. One of my co-workers placed this sign on the reluctant vendor: "Kick the Habit—Not the Machine."

—Fred Bimber *(Painesville, Ohio)*

MY HUSBAND'S London business partner comes occasionally to the States. On his last visit here he suffered from a digestive upset and sought out a drugstore. When he asked for a certain remedy, the druggist said, "Oh, you're going abroad."

"No," replied our proper Englishman. "I *am* abroad."

—Mrs. Stuart B. Hartman *(Westport, Conn.)*

IN OUR residential Westchester County community, the roads were laid out with little rhyme or reason. Therefore, it is not unusual for people unfamiliar with the area to get lost. One day, a particularly bewildered-looking driver stopped at my house and asked directions to the Landrys' house. I told him to turn left at the corner, take his first right and look for the third house on the right. Before he drove off, I added that the Landrys had been transferred and did not live there anymore. "Yes, I know," the driver replied sheepishly. "I do."

—J. M. Posen *(Armonk, N.Y.)*

IT HAD been several months since I'd talked with Pete, a Cuban who had come to the States to live. "Do you know what has happened to me since I last saw you?" he asked. "I've become an American citizen!"

I extended my congratulations, and he continued proudly, "You know, I used to think of myself as a Cuban who spoke poor English. Now I'm an American who speaks good Spanish."

—Ken Taylor *(Dallas, Texas)*

Home Sweet Homework!

By WILL STANTON

AT THE school our boys attend, the honor roll is divided into Outstanding Scholarship, Honor Scholarship and Honorable Mention. We were visiting some friends one evening not long ago, and I happened to remark that Roy had made Honorable Mention.

"Yeah?" Al said. "The same thing happened to Curtis a few months back. There was no television for him for some time afterward, I can tell you."

That struck me as being slightly irrational until it finally came out that this was the first time Curtis hadn't made Outstanding Scholarship. Big deal. As I said to Maggie on the way home, "If there's one thing I can't stand, it's parents who brag about their kids' grades!

"What do grades prove anyhow?" I asked. "I'd rather have normal, well-rounded kids like ours. Their only trouble is that they don't apply themselves. There's no reason in the world they can't make Outstanding Scholarship. In fact, from now on I'm going over their homework with them every night."

The next evening, after dinner, I told the boys I wanted to see their homework. "If Curtis can get straight As, there's no reason you two can't."

Sammy pronounced Curtis a dope who never did anything but read and study. I said it was too bad they weren't a little more like him. Roy told me he didn't have anything to do except some spelling, and it wasn't due for another week.

"No time like the present," I said. "Let's see how much you know about spelling. Why, when I was your age, I was almost always first or second in the spelling bees." Roy wanted to know what that was. I said that when people got together to do something special they called it a "bee." "You mean like a party?" he asked.

"You might call it a party," I said. I explained about spelling bees, husking bees, and so on.

He wandered into the next room, and I overheard him talking to Sammy. "You know what they used to do when Dad was a boy," he asked, "when they wanted to have a party? They got a lot of people together and pulled the husks off corn and spelled hard words."

"Man!" Sammy said. "No *wonder* he gets crabby so often."

I decided to drop the spelling work for a while.

THE following evening, I thought I'd see what they knew about history. "What can you tell me about George Washington?"

"He went across the river standing up, and he chopped the cherry tree down," Sammy answered.

"That didn't really happen," Roy added. "It's just a lie somebody made up to teach kids to tell the truth."

"What about Columbus?" I asked. He was an "old-time" discoverer, they thought. That was about it. So I told them about all his voyages, and how he thought he had discovered China. "He wanted to prove you could reach the East by sailing West."

"That's dumb," Roy said. "It's like walking around the block to go next door."

"Or walking around the house to get to the kitchen," Sammy added.

"That's enough," I told them. "You can stop acting so smart. I'll bet Columbus never got a D in social studies."

"Yeah," Sammy said. "But I'll bet he never had Mrs. Hazeltine, either."

"Let's stick to the subject," I said. "His crewmen were scared because they thought that the sea was flat and when the ship got to the edge it would go right over."

Sammy didn't believe it. Roy agreed. "Nobody would believe that. If the ship went over the edge, the water would, too. There wouldn't be any sea."

"*We* know that," I said. "But *they* didn't. They had no idea the world was round."

"Makes no difference," Sammy announced. "You pour

water on a table, and it will run over the edge. Same with the ocean."

"Right," said Roy. "Can't you see that? If the water kept pouring over the edge all those years, where would it go?"

"I didn't say it went anywhere," I replied.

"It would have to," Sammy said. "And that's the reason a flat world won't work."

"Okay, okay," I admitted. "Now, what can you tell me about Columbus?"

"Well," Roy said, "he thought America was China, so he called the people Indians; and on the way home he sank the *Santa Maria,* and for this they named a day after him."

"That's enough history for now," I told them.

THE boys didn't have much trouble with math except for word problems. "Let's try one," I said. "Forty-two Scouts are going to a ball game in seven cars. How many Scouts to a car?" Long silence. "Sammy, you mean to tell me you can't divide seven into 42?"

"Sure," he said. "But how can you divide cars into Scouts?" His teacher kept telling them you can't subtract apples from pears. He wasn't subtracting, I told him. He was dividing, and that was different. He allowed as maybe it would work with cars but not with buses. I told him not to be ridiculous. He kept insisting. "All right," I said, "give me a problem and we'll try it."

He said 393 kids were going to the game, and they had 20 buses. How many to each bus?

"Fine," I said. "Twenty goes into 39 once. Naught from nine is nine..."

"Hold it!" Sammy burst out. "The 20 is buses, and the 393 is kids. You can't subtract."

I looked at the paper. The kid was right. You try to subtract buses from kids and what do you wind up with? I picked up my pencil and went on with the problem. "It comes out to 19 to a bus, with 13 left over."

Sammy stared at me. "You mean those 13 kids don't get to go?"

Roy said probably their mothers would take them. Sammy considered that unfair if all the rest got to go by bus. Roy asked what if they rented another bus? It took me a minute to figure it. "That would make 18 in a bus, with 15 over."

"It keeps getting worse," Roy said.

Sammy thought arithmetic was a crummy subject.

"You can't blame it on arithmetic," I said. "It's doing the best it can." Sammy said that wasn't good enough.

Later, he came downstairs to tell me he'd got it figured out. "All you have to do is borrow six kids from another problem, and rent another bus." I sent him to bed.

ONE afternoon I was looking through Roy's science book and decided to try some of the experiments. The first involved the principle of the windlass, using the pencil sharpener on the kitchen wall. I removed the cover from the sharpener and ran a cord from its axle to a scrub bucket on the floor. Then I showed the boys how to lift the bucket by turning the crank. Roy said big deal, lifting an empty bucket. I said, "Okay, we'll use a full one." Sammy wanted to fill it with water, but I put a stop to that. "Find something that won't make a mess if it spills." Roy put a stack of cookbooks in the bucket and Sammy put in a big bunch of bananas. It added up to a pretty good weight.

Roy started to turn the crank, the cord grew taut, the bucket shifted. And the pencil sharpener came off the wall. "Hey," Sammy said, "it works."

"Yeah," Roy chimed in. "Only how often do you want to take down a pencil sharpener?"

"You don't get the idea," I said. I got some heavier screws and fastened the sharpener more securely to the wall. This time it worked fine. I left the boys taking turns with it. After a minute, Sammy called me back to see their invention. I went over to take a close look. He had the bucket cranked up as high as it would go and was just holding it there.

"So—what is it?" I inquired.

"A power pencil sharpener," Roy said. He shoved a pencil into the slot, Sammy let go the crank—and the bucket fell on my foot.

WHEN Maggie got home from the store she wanted to know why I was limping. "The boys tried to tell me you hurt your foot on an automatic pencil sharpener."

"Just showing the boys a science experiment," I told her. "A bucket fell on it." "An empty bucket?" she asked. "No," I said, "a full one." She went on putting groceries away. "Full of what?" she asked. "Cookbooks and bananas," I said.

She stopped what she was doing and looked at me. "These days you aren't even safe in your own home."

I went over to help with the groceries.

"Do you suppose there's such a thing as giving the boys too much help?" she asked. "I mean, it might make them too dependent?"

I studied a box of cereal. "Maggie, you know what I think I'll do? I think I'll teach the boys to stand on their own two feet—think for themselves. I'm going to let them do their own homework just like my father always let me do mine."

Maggie nodded slowly. "That's the American way," she said.

PARDON, YOUR SLIP IS SHOWING

FROM the Pittsfield, Mass., *Berkshire Eagle:* "The accident occured shortly after 1 P.M. Pickett took his eyes from the road momentarily to look at a trick going in the opposite direction."

FROM the Virginia, Minn., *Mesabi News:* "The school is located on a 14-acre tract, and is resigned to accommodate 600 students."

CLASSIFIED ad in the Spokane, Wash., *Spokesman-Review:* "Two plots in lively Fairmount Cemetery."

FROM a church bulletin: "Ushers will swat late-comers at these points in the service."

—*Vermont Churchman*

"Stow It
Till the Commercial!"

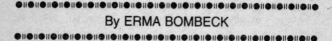

By ERMA BOMBECK

I WAS MARRIED during a beer commercial in the World Series, at which time I promised to love my husband in sickness and in health. But I never agreed to live with a catatonic sports addict.

So I am now in the process of having my husband declared legally dead. This is a test case. If it works, 38 million American housewives, widowed by TV sports, plan to have me canonized. But it won't be easy. My attorneys have informed me that merely proving he sits before a TV with fixed eyes and no pulse won't be enough. They said I would have to keep a log of his behavior for a year. I began this diary one year ago. Here are some monthly highlights:

August

THE 15TH of the month was visiting day for the children. In the glow of the TV I lined them up and said sadly, "Children, this is your father." He offered them a pretzel while watching a baseball game. When we insisted, he stood up. The children remembered him as a much shorter man.

When they left, my husband turned to me. "Who did you say they were?" he asked. "And how come they all talk like Howard Cosell?"

September

ON MY weekly pilgrimage to my husband's lair, I waited quietly until they flashed an instant replay of a dog running across the field chased by an usher. Then I asked, "Do you suppose you could put the screens in today, even if summer is almost over?" He looked at me in disbelief. "What kind of an animal are you? On a day Joe Namath pulls a tendon, you want me to put in the screens?"

October

TODAY, our living room became the first recycling center to be serviced by a mobile unit. My husband was so engrossed in watching the World Series that he was quite unaware of the cub scouts who gathered eight barrels of cans, six barrels of bottles and 500 pounds of paper.

I pecked my husband on the cheek as the boys huffed off. He swatted at me and grumbled, "How did that fly get in here?"

November

IN THE MIDDLE of the Dallas-Los Angeles football game my husband charged into the kitchen. "All right," he demanded, "where is it?"

"Where is what?" I asked.

"The bathroom."

"Down the hall, the second door."

"How long has it been there?"

"Since we moved."

"And why wasn't I told we moved?"

"We *did* tell you. You were watching the "American Sportsman" and Fess Parker was treeing a coon and we said, 'We are going to move.'"

"Do you honestly expect a man to remember anything that is said to him during a coon hunt?" he asked.

December

IT IS NOT EASY to arrange a room around a Christmas tree, a Father figure and the opening of the basketball season.

"Jesse," I said to my son, "pick up your father and put him next to the fireplace. No, that won't work. He's blocking the doorway. Try shoving him over next to the sofa."

"Will Dad be with us this Christmas?" asked one of the children.

"Only if it is the will of the NBA. If you see a star in the East, follow it and try to talk the New York Knicks out of playing on Christmas Day."

January

THE WINTER has not been kind to what's-his-name. You can't watch 15 bowl games and emerge unscathed. He is annoyed when anything but sports action flashes on the tube. He even made an obscene phone call to Betty White for delaying *his game* with the Rose Bowl parade.

February

HAVING READ that man does not live by Curt Gowdy alone, I slid into my sexiest night apparel, dabbed perfume behind each ear and slithered into the living room. He was watching a Rangers' game.

I perched on the arm of his chair and asked huskily, "Wanta nibble on my ear?" "Why?" he mumbled. "Isn't there any more chip dip?"

March

ALL THE green things are coming out this month, except my husband. He is being fed intravenously on a diet of basketball, pre-season baseball, golf and hockey.

It has become a game with the family to think of ways to get Daddy out of the chair. We have tried, "Your sweater is on fire," "You have just won the Nobel Prize for Boredom," and "I am leaving. You get custody of the kids." We have not yet found the right shock treatment.

April

THROUGH a conscientious program of throat massage, and stuffing his mouth with pebbles, we were able to get my husband up to four words a day during the period before the baseball season began.

The first day he said, "Wha..."

The second day he said, "What."

The third day he said, "What is your name?"

Then the season started, and he regressed once more to clearing his throat.

May

FOR Mother's Day, we put Grandma in knee socks, shin guards and a hockey mask, and shoved her in front of his chair. He was watching a roller-derby re-run, and granted her an audience for only a few seconds. Then he punched her playfully on the arm and said, "Hang in there, kid!"

June

IN AN attempt to take our Christmas tree down, I inadvertently blocked his view of Jimmy Connors returning a lob.

"Good grief, woman," he said, "will you let that poor tree alone and get out of here?"

"It's a Christmas tree," I said, "and it has been dropping needles since December."

"Which is exactly the way our ecology was planned. Now get out of there. Jimmy abhors distractions."

July

"I AM leaving you," I said calmly. "I can't stand it any more—the loneliness, the boredom, the roller derbies, the golf tournaments, the snacks. I'm young. I have all my teeth. I want to dance and drink champagne from a slipper. Do you understand?"

"Shhhh," he said. "There's a commercial coming up. Can you stow it till then?"

Somehow, I got the feeling this is where I came in.

JUMPING TO CONFUSIONS

MOTHER scolding her three offspring: "Oh, you three are a pair, if ever there was one!"

—Contributed by Evelyn Gratton

WHILE we were looking over some items in a department store, the sales clerk said helpfully, "If you see something that isn't there, we probably have more in the back."

—Contributed by David A. Cowdrick, Jr.

A MAN joined a group at a bus stop and asked, "Has the next bus gone yet?"

—Contributed by W. Moffat

All in a Day's Work II

MY FATHER, who is a wholesaler, says that the fastest way to get merchandise from a manufacturer is to cancel the order. This is confirmed by a telegram he received after sending a cancellation notice. The wire read: CANNOT CANCEL. HAVE SHIPPED TOMORROW.

—Contributed by Mary Van Ostenberg

MY OFFICE WINDOW in Liverpool, England, overlooks dockyard gates through which enter numerous trucks carrying huge quantities of refined salt for export. Negotiating the sharp turn through the gates is difficult, and one truck mounted the curb, causing several sacks of salt to fall off into the road, where they burst open.

The driver got out to survey the damage. Then, checking to see if he was being observed, he grabbed some of the loose salt and threw it over his left shoulder.

—Contributed by W. R. Macrae

I WAS at a post-operative meeting for recent open-heart-surgery patients and relatives at the Cleveland Clinic Foundation Hospital. The surgeon, explaining some of the procedures of coronary arterial grafts and artificial heart valves, stated that he and his colleagues were really just plumbers. One voice gasped from the audience, "Good Lord! Your fees won't be *that* high, will they?"

—Contributed by Donald Kemp

Toward More
Picturesque Speech III

Comparing Notes

As self-sacrificing as a candle

(Angie Papadakis)

Talk Show

Out of the mouths of babes come words we shouldn't have said in the first place

(Ruth E. Renkel)

Close Ups

His huff arrived and he departed in it

(Alexander Woollcott)

He received the news with his eyebrows

(John Galsworthy)

Character Reference

Dr. Jekyll had something to Hyde

(Robert Fuoss)

Cyclops had 20 vision

(Shelby Friedman)

Yoga and Me

●॥●॥●॥●॥●॥●॥●॥●॥●॥●॥●॥●॥●॥●॥●॥●॥●॥●॥●

By FLOYD MILLER

●॥●॥●॥●॥●॥●॥●॥●॥●॥●॥●॥●॥●॥●॥●॥●॥●॥●॥●

MY WIFE talks at breakfast. Pavlov could have learned all about conditioned reflexes from Meg without fussing with all those dogs; just place a poached egg in front of her and she talks. But since I'm not very well tuned in at that hour, we tend to have faulty communication.

"Yoga was taught centuries ago in India, the Himalayas and Tibet," she said one morning.

"Always thought yogurt was a Jewish dish," I muttered.

"Put down your newspaper," she said sternly.

I put down the paper to discover that she had been reading from a leaflet, which she now waved under my nose. "A yogi has moved to town and is giving lessons in yoga. The yogi is the practitioner or teacher; yoga is the Hindu philosophy of exercise and health. It gets rid of the flab and gives spiritual tranquillity. I think a few lessons would be good for you."

She dropped the leaflet in front of me. It contained a picture of the yogi, half-naked and in a terrible situation. One leg was wrapped around his neck; the other was tucked under an armpit; his arms were cruelly twisted behind his back.

"Good Lord, who did that to him?" I demanded.

Undaunted, Meg went on. "He has a class Thursday morning at his home. He says he can fit you in."

"Well, you just tell him to unfit me. If you think I'm going to sit around in a loincloth and study my navel..."

"I bought you a new pair of white tennis shorts. You'll look just fine."

That evening I found the shorts laid out on my bed. Simply out of curiosity, I tried them on and stepped in front of the

177

full-length mirror. *This* was me? Chest concave . . . stomach protruding . . . a flabby roll of flesh spilling over the waistband of the shorts! When had this happened?

I arrived 15 minutes before class time on Thursday morning. The yogi greeted me rather absentmindedly and led me into a large living room with thick oriental carpets on the floor. A few minutes later, a lovely blonde entered the room to be introduced as Mrs. Nancy Something-or-other. Soon we were joined by Barbara, Alice, Connie, Dorothy and Vicky. With a touch of panic I realized that this was the total class: six girls in their late 20s, and me!

Some distant chime announced 9:30—class time—and at this moment a startling thing happened: all the girls began to strip off their clothes. Was yoga secretly performed in the nude? My hands clutched protectively at my new tennis shorts. After discarding their blouses and skirts, my classmates weren't nude after all. Under their clothes they were wearing leotards.

Leotards, I discovered, are a sort of glamorous long underwear. Being silky and elastic, they dramatically displayed every detail of the girls' personal geography. With some terrible perverseness I kept studying the pattern in one of the rugs instead of looking where I wanted to look. I was in my 50s—wasn't this supposed to be a dangerous age? I tried to feel dangerous, but it eluded me. I tried acting debonair, then avuncular, finally jaded. None of the acts worked. I could feel only like a bumbler.

The yogi called the class to order, and we formed two rows facing him. I took a position at the far end of the second row, where I would be least observed. Close by on my right were Dorothy, Connie and Alice. The yogi placed the palms of his hands together in the attitude of prayer, and we all sat on the floor in the Lotus position. This looked simple enough when the yogi assumed it: he merely crossed his legs, entwined them under him and tucked his heels up in his groin. Closing his eyes, he said, "The great secret of life is the achievement of action through non-action."

I was having difficulties. I got my legs crossed, but couldn't get my heels tucked up because my knees wouldn't go down; they remained a good eight inches above the floor. Since the other members of the class had their eyes closed, I decided to cheat a little and, placing my hand on my right knee, I pressed down hard. The knee went to the floor all right, but I tipped over. Finding my head in her lap, Dorothy let out a startled cry—whereupon all eyes opened and stared at me. "I fell over," I mumbled as I righted myself.

This ended the period of meditation. Now the yogi said, "The study of yoga can take many paths, but we will pursue Hatha Yoga, in order to purify and strengthen the body systems by exercises and controlled breathing. *Ha* means the flow of breath through the right nostril, *tha* the flow through the left, and *yoga* signifies the union of the two. Absolute Energy, the Life Force, is contained within everything. It is called Prana, and we induce it into all parts of our bodies by controlled breathing."

We all began taking deep breaths. I might be a lousy Lotus, but I was a pretty good breather, and I filled my lungs with so much Prana that I felt dizzy.

After several more exercises, the yogi announced a rest period. Here was something I *had* to be good at.

"Lie flat on your backs and imagine that you are in a secluded flower garden," the yogi intoned. "A fragrance fills the air . . . a soft breeze caresses you . . . you are relaxing, relaxing . . . breathe slow . . . slow . . . you are drowsy . . ."

I turned my head slowly to the right and actually saw a beautiful landscape of soft hills and valleys, a series of them. Then I realized that they were Dorothy, Connie and Alice. I was in the wrong garden!

As we neared the end of the session at 11 o'clock, I had a record of 100-percent failure. The yogi could no longer bring himself to look in my direction; the rest of the class acted as if I didn't exist. To be a non-person is discouraging, I found.

The yogi gave an enigmatic smile and said, "We do the headstand."

The headstand is done by each student individually, while the yogi stands close by to encourage and assist. It is difficult, until the body has been prepared by exercise.

"The headstand reverses the pull of gravity on our body," the yogi was saying. "It sends the blood to the head and stimulates the mind, tones up the nervous system, increases sexual powers."

My hand shot in the air as I volunteered to perform this demanding feat. The yogi looked at me in disbelief; Nancy and Barbara and Alice and Connie and Dorothy and Vicky looked at me in disbelief. "The position should be approached with caution by anyone over, ah, 40," the yogi said. My hand stayed aloft. He had given me an easy out, but my hand wouldn't take it.

With the yogi instructing me, I knelt down on the thick carpet, interlaced my fingers and placed my forearms on the floor to form a small cage into which I was told to place my head. I straightened my legs and walked toward my head until I could go no farther. Now all I had to do was kick my legs into the air and hold them straight up. I kicked, but they went only a few inches off the floor. I kicked again. They went a bit higher, but came thudding back down at once. The room was silent as I prepared a final assault on the forces of gravity. With a mighty thrust I flung my legs into the air—and they stayed there!

"...two...three...four..." I heard the yogi counting off the seconds. Ten seconds was the goal. I began to wobble. "...five...six..." I thrashed my legs to recapture my balance, but on the count of seven I came crashing down. There was a strange clattering sound in my head: to my amazement, as I sat up, I discovered the entire class looking at me admiringly and applauding. A seven-second headstand was remarkable, the girls all said. And when the class broke up, they all smiled at me as they put their clothes back on and said we'd see each other again next week. As I walked to my car, I found that the exercises had toned me up; I really did feel better.

"How'd it go?" my wife asked when I arrived home.

"Pretty good," I said, careful not to overplay it.

"Who's in the class?"

"Oh, a half-dozen assorted people. Nobody we know." I was being very careful to tell the truth.

"You going to continue the class?"

I patted her hand and said, "If you want me to."

"I do, dear. I can see improvement in you already."

I nodded judiciously. "There may well be something in this yoga business."

The following afternoon, I overheard a telephone conversation between my wife and one of her friends. I heard Meg say, "Oh, he'll continue the lessons, never fear. I arranged for him to be in a class of young women."

I was angry at my wife's deceit. It would have served her right if I quit the lessons. But, after careful thought, I decided I couldn't be that petty. Yoga teaches us to be generous to the unenlightened.

A Little Suit for Hymie

By HARRY GOLDEN

WHEN DID YOU buy a winter suit, or a heavy overcoat? In the middle of the summer, of course. In the summer you could maybe pick up a bargain—a good suit or an overcoat which the fellow had not sold the previous winter. And so the hotter the day the better.

You wanted to take along as many members of the family as possible. You left nothing to chance. The word went down: "We are buying Hymie a winter suit"; and the matter was prepared carefully.

It had to be on a Sunday because of the "mayvinn." A mayvinn is a connoisseur. Every family had a mayvinn; usually an uncle or a cousin who was a presser in a pants factory and who knew all about cloth and workmanship.

Finally you are all set. Everybody is there, the mother, the father, the oldest brother, the mayvinn and, of course, 13-year-old Hymie, who is to get the first suit bought expressly for him, a blue serge suit which he is to wear for the first time on the High Holy Days the following October. The mayvinn always knew "a place" where a bargain could be had. So the family set out and the mayvinn led the party down the street and inside the establishment.

The mother picked a stool and seated herself at a point where her eyes could sweep the stairway to the basement, the front door, the mirror, the sales force and the platform where Hymie, the victim, was to stand. The salesman started a big spiel, and everyone let the mother do the talking. Her attitude was always challenging, almost belligerent. She raised her arm and said, "Never mind the talk; all we want here is a little suit for a bar-mitzvah boy."

The idea was always to minimize the project; use the word "little" as often as possible, and the religious overtones, "bar mitzvah," couldn't hurt, even though the salesman had heard it a hundred times that week end.

The father, older brother and the mayvinn took their places to the right of the platform. Hymie was already standing there with his pants off. The salesman said, "I've got just what you want," and started toward the basement steps. He had a thousand suits on the floor, but he always went to the basement. This gave him a good talking point—the suit was special. But the mother countered with: "What are you going to bring us, something you are ashamed to keep on the floor?" This was good. It took the edge off the salesman's early advantage. Now he would have to expend precious talk in merely trying to recover.

Presently he returned, carrying a blue serge suit. The father, the older brother and the mother instinctively looked toward the mayvinn. They want him to be on the alert.

Now the salesman helps Hymie with the pants, then the coat, smooths it out in the back, and, as he's standing behind the boy, the mother lands another good blow: "What are you doing there behind the boy? Let him stand by himself; we'll see what's what." The salesman walks away, but recovers with a solid punch: "I was saving this suit for my own nephew, for his own bar mitzvah, but when I saw such a handsome boy come in I had to bring it up."

Now the mayvinn steps forward. "Take off the coat." Hymie takes off the coat. The mayvinn goes out the door, into the light. Everybody is watching except Hymie, who is sitting on the floor until the mother sees him. "Stand up and don't dirty the pants; we're not buying this suit—yet," and the salesman sighs.

Meanwhile the mayvinn holds the coat up to the sun. He feels it. His hands go into the pockets. He rubs the cloth between his fingers. Then he brings the coat in. The salesman leans forward. Even Hymie is tense. Everybody looks at the mayvinn. He is deliberate in his decison. He finally says, "Not a bad piece of goods"—the highest compliment. The mother looks with contempt; "Also a mayvinn," she says, but she knows the salesman now has the upper hand.

Things are coming to a climax. The slightest inflection of

the voice can have serious consequences. The mother tries to be nonchalant: "How much for this secondhand suit which you were not able to sell to anybody all winter long?"

The mother has regained the initiative. Now the salesman has to fight back. "What do you mean, secondhand, and we couldn't sell it all winter long?" But the mother senses the kill and does not let him continue. "All right, so why do you still have a winter suit on the hottest day in the summer?" The salesman begins, "Listen, lady . . ." but the mother follows up her advantage, "How much?" The salesman is groggy. Now he becomes belligerent and fairly yells, "Fifty dollars." A mistake. The mother had goaded him too much. "Fifty dollars?" the father and the mayvinn say in unison, and then the mother begins to laugh, which is the signal for everybody else to laugh; everybody except the salesman and Hymie, who wants to know, "Where is the toilet?"

When the salesman shows him, the mother delivers another blow—"Watch out for the pants, Hymie. We are going someplace else."

When Hymie comes back he takes off the suit and the mother stands up and starts walking out. They all follow her. The salesman catches up with the party on the sidewalk. The mother shakes her head. "There's nothing to talk about. If you said maybe 35 dollars, we would think you were crazy," she says. They keep walking. Now the mayvinn is catching hell. "'Not a bad piece of goods,' he says; who needed you?" They go to two other stores, but this is only a bit of East Side protocol. They would never have forgiven themselves if they had made the purchase without "looking around." Finally, between four and five o'clock, they come back to the first store.

Only the mother goes in. The salesman tries to act surprised. Actually he expected them to return. She now becomes palsy-walsy with the salesman—"All right, take the 35 dollars and let the boy have a nice suit for his bar mitzvah." The salesman whispers, "So help me, I am doing something against my own flesh and blood when I give you this suit for 40 dollars." The deal is closed and they go home, tired but very, very happy.

The mother takes her place in the kitchen to make potato *latkes* for everyone. And she resumes her traditional status within the family circle—"Hymie, did you give your father a big kiss for the suit he bought you today?"

Camp Sights

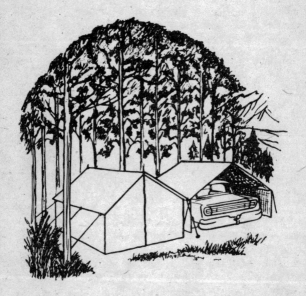

"I had the most awful nightmare last night."
NAT, MASTERS AGENCY

"Tent poles? I thought they were firewood."
BO BROWN, KING FEATURES

"Now I know why your mother thought this was the perfect place to camp!"

FRANK BAGINSKI IN *FAMILY WEEKLY*

"I can't help thinking how we could be staying in the finest hotel on what it's costing us to board the dogs."

DUNAGIN, PUBLISHERS-HALL SYNDICATE

"What are these lipstick marks on the refrigerator and stove?"

BOB BARNES, REGISTER AND TRIBUNE SYNDICATE

A Definition of Marriage

By OGDEN NASH

How wise I am to have instructed the butler
    to instruct the first footman to instruct
    the second footman to instruct the door-
    man to order my carriage:
I am about to volunteer a definition of
    marriage.
Just as I know that there are two Hagens,
    Walter and Copen,
I know that marriage is a legal and religious
    alliance entered into by a man who
    can't sleep with the window shut and a
    woman who can't sleep with the
    window open,
Also he can't sleep until he has read the last
    hundred pages to find out whether his
    suspicions of the murdered eccentric
    recluse's avaricious secretary were
    right,
And she can't sleep until he puts out the light,
Which when he finally does she is still awake
    and turns on hers,
And if he thinks she's going to turn it off
    before she finds out whether Janis
    marries the shy young clergyman or the
    sophisticated polo player, he errs.
Moreover, just as I am unsure of the
    difference between flora and fauna, and
    flotsam and jetsam,

I am quite sure that marriage is the alliance of
       two people, one of whom never
       remembers birthdays and the other
       never forgetsam,
And the one refuses to believe there is a leak
       in the water pipe or the gas pipe, and
       the other is convinced she is about to
       asphyxiate or drown,
And the other says, "Quick, get up and get
       my hairbrushes off the window sill; it's
       raining in," and the one replies, "Oh,
       they're all right; it's only raining
       straight down."
That is why marriage is so much more
       interesting than divorce,
Because it's the only known example of the
       happy meeting of the immovable object
       and the irresistible force.
So I hope husbands and wives will continue
       to debate and combat over everything
       debatable and combatable,
Because I believe a little incompatibility is the
       spice of life, particularly if he has
       income and she is pattable.

ACUTE SHORTAGE

AFTER I EMIGRATED to Canada from India, I applied for a job.
During my first interview, I was very nervous. When the interviewer asked me why I wanted a job with his firm, I was
baffled for a moment. Finally I blurted out, "There are too
many chiefs in your company and not enough Indians!"

    I was hired.

                          —Contributed by Gnanendrap Murugan

Kitchen Graffiti

By DOLORES CURRAN

SOME FAMILIES talk together, but most of the families I know communicate by writing notes. I'm convinced that anthropologists will someday interpret our culture from the notes we leave around our homes, just as we study past family life from cave paintings.

Will the sociologists of the future read our families by the location of the notes? Well, the families who leave their notes on the kitchen counter or table either eat out all the time or are compulsive housekeepers. I can't imagine a more unlikely place for a note to be found than on *our* kitchen counter. There isn't room, what with the blender, mixer, coffeepot, canisters, cream puffs, the pile of untried recipes—not to mention Gregory's Little League schedule, Marty's pedometer and Dad's early tomato plants.

We belong to that great American class of refrigerator note pasters. I guess that tells you where our values lie. We also paste our kids' artwork on the refrigerator. If you cover the enamel with proud poster paintings, you don't have to wash the outside of the refrigerator for years.

Since ours is a normal family passing through the kitchen on its way to life, we each write at least one note a day. A typical day's sampling goes like this:

Mom: pick me up at 3:28. I have a student council before basketball practice but need to be at the library anyway. Allison.

I used to try to figure out notes like that, but now I just obey them. Rationality confuses family life.

Mom—we're out of milk and jerky. Another handwriting: *and notebook paper.*

Notebook paper? That's groceries?

MOMDONTFORGETTOMAKECUBSCOUTCOOKIES.

YOURSONTOM.

Dolor—better put gas in the car. I think it's low. Jim.

He was right. I found that out driving a car pool to school.

Poly—Jodie or Joey called. Wants to borrow your red skirt or shirt. She forgot to leave her number but call her right away. Steve.

And so on. This is the stuff of which families are made, not sibling rivalry and such-like family relationships as sociologists hold. Not culture and genes as anthropologists hold. No. In essence, family is homely things like appointments, bikes, gas, and basketball practice. The family that writes together communicates together today.

Maybe we need a course in our parenting on how to write notes. I used to correct grammar and spelling, but they started writing on such tiny scraps of paper that there wasn't room. But they could use help in how to get the basic message across, not garbled like this one:

Mom—Press the flowers this afternoon. Mike.

Baffled, I researched it and discovered that my bookseller had the book I ordered: *Hope for the Flowers* by Paulist Press and would be open until 5 that afternoon.

On the other hand, a child can get down too much, as in this note:

Mom—Mrs. Olson called at 11 o'clock and wanted to tell you that her aunt is coming from Minneapolis next Thursday into Stapleton Airport because her mother is sick at Swedish Hospital and so she won't be able to go on the field trip so can you? Love, Andy.

Andy was in second grade and a very slow printer at the time. Imagine the length of that conversation!

Whenever people decry the lack of family communication today, I get nervous. Sometimes we have too much of it. But lately we've been more creative. One note led to a chain:

We're out of lemons

If somebody hands you a lemon make lemonade

Make lemonade out of my brother

Why Not you DESERVE A TREAT TODAY

Oh are you going away agen

Again Weirdo, not Agen when are you going to learn to spell

You shouldn't talk that way to Mom!

Don't bring me into this. What do you want lemons for anyway?

You blew it Sis, Remember I didn't tell.

Once upon a family I would have lined them up and found out what they didn't tell. Now I'd rather not know. I just wrote this note:

There are lemons in the refrigerator. Use them immediately I don't want to know what for.

Mom

In disguised penmanship, this message was appended to my note:

NEVER END A SENTENCE WITH A PREPOSITION

How do you write a sigh?

Campus Comedy

IN HIS first class at an eastern university, a guest professor from France was aghast when several coeds calmly took out knitting bags and began to ply their needles. He could hardly finish the hour. By the time the class met again, however, he was ready with a solution.

"I have an important announcement to make," he said when the final bell rang. Then, as everyone quieted down expectantly, he continued, "It is simply this—only those young ladies will be permitted to knit in class who are pregnant." There was no more knitting in his classes.

—Contributed by Howard N. Meyer

TWO MOTHERS were discussing their respective daughters, both about to enter college. "What is your daughter taking?" asked one. "Seventeen skirts and 34 blouses!" the other answered.

—Contributed by Mrs. Jack Hill

A DARTMOUTH English professor who had traveled extensively took professional pride in correctly pronouncing the names of his foreign students. One year, on the opening day of the fall term, the professor began his class by calling the roll of students, reading all their names carefully as usual. Each answered promptly except a Mr. Blu-esky. There was no response when the professor called out this apparently Slavic name.

After class a dark-haired young man approached the professor and asked why his name had not been called. "What is your name?" the professor asked. "Blue Sky," answered the student, adding, "I am an American Indian."

—Contributed by Eugene Jaroshevich

A MATH professor at the University of Alabama, who had become a father for the first time, assumed the care of the infant one evening when his wife wasn't feeling well. Came diaper-changing time, and after struggling interminably with the triangle he finally cried out, "Mary, which side does the hypotenuse go on?"

—Contributed by Camille M. Elebash

SIGN in the administration office of a Colorado college: "FRESHMAN ENGLISH SPOKEN HERE."

—Contributed by H. Gordon Hilden

BEING struck by a wordy muse, a friend of mine concluded her paper for a Shakespeare course with the statement: "Pusillanimity was, to the end, his downfall." When the paper was returned, her professor had added: "As obfuscation is thine."

—Contributed by Kim H. Parker

DURING a lecture in geography at Northwest Missouri State College, the professor was explaining that the term "backward" is no longer used when describing the economy of a primitive state. In order to avoid hurting the pride of such countries, the term "underdeveloped" is considered preferable. Looking around the lecture hall, he saw one student who didn't seem to understand the psychological implications of the two words. "Well, Miss Turner," he asked, "which would you rather be—underdeveloped or backward?"

Her quick reply to the red-faced professor: "Backward, sir!"

—Contributed by Larry L. Young

AT THE END of my sophomore year at Indiana State University, my mother, a widow, decided to attend summer school to get an extension on her teaching license. This meant that I would have to stay at home to keep an eye on the house. At first, I was worried about how the return to college life would affect her. After a week, I received a letter which read: "Dear John, How is everything? I have met the nicest guy. Please send money. Love, Mother." I never worried another minute.

—Contributed by John Freeman

How I Spread Happiness Without Really Trying

By WILL STANTON

WE CAN'T all be President, can't all play Hamlet, can't all build the Taj Mahal. But we can all make someone happy. Life's finest achievement. Philosophers all agree. Books written on the subject. A smile, kind word, helping hand. Doesn't cost anything.

Some of us can make people happy without even intending to. I've always been lucky in this respect. Gifted, some might say.

A while back, I went into a store to get a cigarette lighter. Salesgirl was at the other end of the counter talking to friends. Laughing. Snapping fingers. Enjoying life. Cleared my throat. Girl ignored me. I became annoyed; rapped on counter. Girl sauntered over. Chewing gum. Sullen. Large hairdo with tiny opening for face. Like baby bird peeking out of nest. I spoke to her of responsibility to store. Service. Dedication. Loud enough for others to hear.

"I don't want to seem too critical," I said. "But you're being paid to wait on customers, not to visit with friends. A person with minimal skills and training can make up for it by being extra courteous and helpful. I suggest that in the future you spend less time having fun and more time earning your salary."

Girl visibly shaken. Remorseful. Rang up purchase. Told me $2.85. I reached for money. No money. Wallet in other pants. Explained to girl. Girl smiled.

Remarkable change. Entire personality suffused by inner glow. She smiled at me again. Smiled at her friends. Radiant.

Salespeople are human. Appreciate customer who takes interest. I left store. Didn't really need lighter. Use matches.

Went to PTA meeting the other evening. Dull. Program chairman requested volunteers to study president's program and make report at next meeting. Lot of mumbling. Hem and haw. Nobody willing to speak out. Stood up. Said I was prepared to make report right then.

Said in my opinion president had no program. All talk and no action. Promises, promises. Spending money like water. Time to think of who's footing the bill. Discussed budget. Postal service. Food and Drug Act. Tax loopholes. Electoral College. Oil depletion. Air pollution. Legal holidays. Other remarks. Talked about 20 minutes. Possibly half-hour. Audience very attentive.

Program chairman thanked me for offering views. Asked for additional volunteers to study president's program. Turned out chairman was referring to PTA president's hot-lunch program. People more relaxed and jolly after that. Several told me best meeting they ever attended. Glad to do my part.

Children got to cutting up the other day. Yelling. Punching. Spilling pop. Throwing filled doughnuts. Sat them down. Took away filled doughnuts. Told them this was serious matter. Waited for silence. Started lecture. Got hiccups.

"We are all judged by the way we beha-!-ve," I told them. "If we act like la-!-dies and gentlemen, we will be treated with re-!-spect." Took deep breath. Held it long time. Resumed lecture. "This may seem like a big joke to you, but bad manners and rudeness are nothing to l-!-augh at. I hope you'll th-!-ink—"

Let them go. Didn't want to overdo. Could see by look on faces that they were impressed. Lips trembling. Unable to look me in the eye. Soon as over, broke into hysterical laughter. Good sign. Release of nervous tension. Relieves frustrations. Children appreciate firmness. Well-disciplined child is happy child. Mine rolling on floor. Sound of child's laughter is golden.

When my wife was in hospital with our last baby, her mother came to stay. After hospital visiting hours Saturday night, I stopped to see friends on way home. Joe and Sheila.

Had couple of drinks. Told them all about baby. How nice, Sheila said. Atmosphere seemed a little tense. Finally, Joe reported cat was on roof. Had climbed tree, jumped across. Couldn't get down.

"She's been there over two hours," Sheila said. "Joe won't do a thing about it."

"Bad back," Joe said. "Not going to climb slippery roof in rain for any damn cat."

Had another drink. Nobody said much. Sat there listening to cat. Meow meow. Pathetic. Hard on nerves. Said *I'd* get cat. Sheila said no. If Joe didn't have enough. . . . Didn't say what. Freshened drink. Still heard cat. "I'll do it," I said.

Roof was in two sections. Lower part no problem. Cat was on upper part. High. Steep. Couldn't make it. Stood on lower part and called, "Here, kitty; nice kitty." Cat immobile. More forceful methods needed. Asked Joe if he had any fish.

Handed me up can of tuna. Tossed pieces toward cat. Couldn't get them close enough. Should have had chunk style. Shredded style okay for salad; doesn't throw worth a damn. Used up whole can. No dice. Cat still parked next to chimney. Meow meow. Decided call it quits. Wrenched knee getting down.

Joe poured a drink. "Should be interesting in the morning," he said, "when sun hits the tuna." No comment from Sheila.

Drove home. Contemplative mood. Mother-in-law waiting at door. Told me friends from Detroit had stopped in. Told them I should be home any minute. Waited three hours.

I said, "I see." Took off coat. Started taking off rubbers. Wasn't wearing any. Took off shoes. Touchy situation. No place for sleazy thinking. Wife in hospital. Husband comes home 2 A.M. Wet. Limping. Strong aroma Scotch and tuna fish. Question: Should I try to sell mother-in-law kitty-kitty story? Inner voice says no. Why borrow trouble?

Told her I stopped in bar. Got talking with blonde. Lost track of time. Said that was as far as things went. Knew it was wrong. Regretted deeply. Lonely man seeking companionship.

She nodded. Said she suspected something of the sort. "Certainly can't approve of what you've done," she said. "It was thoughtless. Inconsiderate."

"Weak," I said. "Selfish. Stupid."

"True," she said. Sat down. Humming. Looked at me kindly. "I'm glad you decided to make a clean breast of it," she said. "I think we both feel better."

Told her *I* did. It was true. Felt much better. Lesson here for all. Spread enough happiness around and some will rub off on you.

"This Is a Recording...."

By BILL VAUGHAN

"HELLO, Sutforth's Dry Goods?"

This is Sutforth's Dry Goods, your wish our command. This is a recording. When you hear the tone please wait one second then place your order. (Blap . . . followed by several seconds of silence.) *Thank you for calling Sutforth's. This is a recording.*

"Will you say that again, please?"

This is Sutforth's Dry Goods, your wish our command. This is a recording. When you hear the tone please wait one second then place your order. (Blap . . . followed by several seconds of silence.) *Thank you for calling Sutforth's. This is a recording.*

"You're not a recording. Instead of saying, 'This *is* Sutforth's,' the second time you emphasized the *this*. I ought to know a recording when I hear one; it's all I ever get. You are a real, live person."

This is Sutforth's . . .

"Shut up. (Aside) Hey, Francine, come listen to this. I've got a real, live person on the telephone. I am not kidding. It is not another of my jokes. Listen . . ."

This is Sutforth's Dry Goods, your wish our command. This is a recording. When you hear the tone please wait one second then place your order. (Blap . . . followed by several seconds of silence.) *Thank you for calling Sutforth's. This is a recording.*

"You are a person. A human being with dandruff and gallstones and who-knows-what-all, like everybody else. I can hear you breathing. (Aside) Francine, couldn't you hear the breathing? What do you mean, you're not sure? It was huh-huh-huh. Breathing, like I haven't heard on a telephone in years. I tell you there is a human hand holding that phone! Listen again."

This is Sutforth's Dry Goods, your wish our command. This is a recording. When you hear the tone please wait one second. . . .

"I know you. You're old man Sutforth and you're drunk. Or you're too cheap to fix your recorder. What's the matter with you, Sutforth? (Aside) What do you mean it doesn't sound like old man Sutforth? I go bowling with him every week and he breathes just that way—huh-huh-huh."

This is Sutforth's . . .

"Cut it out, Sutforth. If I wanted to talk to you I'd see you at the bowling alley. Why don't you admit that you are just pretending to be a recording. Speak up like a man."

. . . Thank you for calling Sutforth's. This is a recording.

"All right, Sutforth, you've gone too far this time."

CLICK.

"Hello, police department? I want to report a fiendish scheme by old man Sutforth, trying to drive me as batty as he is by pretending to be a recording."

This is your police department. When you hear the tone state the nature of your complaint. This is a recording.

"Clancy? Sergeant Clancy. That's you. I can hear you breathing. Pretending to be a recording. It's a plot to unhinge my mind. Real people answering telephones. (Aside) Call the psychiatrist, Francine. You already have? What did he say? A *recording* answered? You fool. It wasn't a recording. It was the doctor pretending to be a recording."

CLICK.

"Lie down? A cool cloth? The green-and-white capsule? Thank you, dear."

Marriage-Go-Round

"That yellow scum on top happens to be Hollandaise sauce."

GRAHAM IN *PUNCH*, (ROTHCO) ©

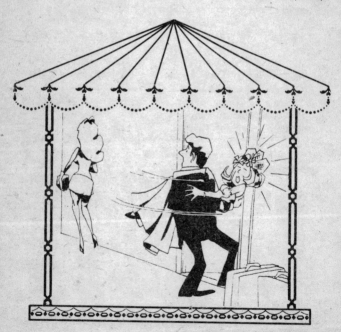

HOEST IN *THE SATURDAY EVENING POST*

"Can't we just once have an argument
without you verifying everything?"

"Alice, what in the world happened?"

JOSEPH FAHRIS. CHICAGO TRIBUNE NEW YORK NEWS SYNDICATE

It's Only a Game

●◎I●I◎I●I◎I●I◎I●I◎I●I◎I●I◎I●I◎I●I◎I●I◎I●I◎I●I◎I●I◎I●I◎I●

By SHIRLEY JACKSON

●◎I●I◎I●I◎I●I◎I●I◎I●I◎I●I◎I●I◎I●I◎I●I◎I●I◎I●I◎I●I◎I●I◎I●

THE LITTLE LEAGUE is new in our town this year, which may
be why my friend Dot and I were so ill-prepared on the day
of the first game. We established ourselves on a little hill near
the third-base line and looked complacently down on the neat
little field our husbands had helped build. Dot asked me if I
remembered the rules of baseball and I said well, I knew both
our boys were on the team with dark-blue hats named the
Braves, and my son Laurie had been coaching me.

"It's so good for the boys to get in on something like this,"
I said.

"Learning sportsmanship and all," Dot said.

"I was telling Laurie last night," I said, "that it doesn't
matter *who* wins, so long as the game is well played."

"It's only a game, after all," Dot said.

"That's what Laurie told me," I said. ("It's only a game,"
he had said, "try to remember, for heaven's sakes, it's only
a game.")

Presently Marian, a friend of ours whose boy Art was first
baseman for the opposing Giants, came along and we offered
her part of our blanket. Then suddenly, from far down the
block, we heard the high-school band playing and everyone
stood up to watch it come onto the field. The ballplayers were
marching behind the band, tall and proud. The sky was blue
and the sun was bright and the boys lined up in their bright
new uniforms, holding their caps while the band played "The
Star-Spangled Banner" and the flag was raised.

"If you cry, I'll tell Laurie," Dot said.

"Same to you," I said, blinking.

After a minute I was able to make out that Laurie was playing second base. I told Marian that I was relieved that Laurie was not pitching, since he had been so nervous anyway, and Marian said that the Giants' manager had insisted on putting Artie at first base because he was dependable.

"I'm sure he'll do very nicely," I said, trying to sound enthusiastic.

It turned out that Billy was playing first base for the Braves, and Marian leaned past me to tell Dot that first base was a *very* responsible position, but she was certain that Billy would play as well as he could. She smiled in what I thought was a nasty kind of way and said she hoped the best team would win. Dot and I smiled back and said we hoped so too. Then the umpire shouted, "Play ball!"

The first Giant batter hit a triple, although, as my husband explained later, it would actually have been an easy infield out if the shortstop had been looking, and if he had thrown the ball anywhere near Billy at first. By the time Billy got the ball back into the infield the batter—Jimmie Hill, who had once borrowed Laurie's bike and brought it back with a flat tire—was on third. I could see Laurie out there banging his hands together, and he looked so pale I was worried.

The Giants made six runs in the first inning, and each time they scored Marian looked sympathetic and told us that really the boys were being quite good sports about it, weren't they? When Laurie bobbled an easy fly she said to me that Artie had told her Laurie was really quite a good ballplayer and I mustn't blame him for an occasional error.

By the time the Giants were finally retired, Marian had told everyone sitting near us that it was her boy who had slid home for the sixth run, and she had explained with great kindness that Dot and I had sons on the other team—the first baseman who had missed that long throw and the second baseman who had dropped the fly ball.

Then the Braves came to bat. Little Ernie Harrow, who lunched frequently at our house, hit the first pitched ball for a fast grounder. It went right through the legs of the Giant center fielder, and when Ernie came dancing into second Dot remarked to Marian that if Artie had been playing closer to first the way Billy did he might have been ready for the throw if the Giant center fielder had managed to stop the ball.

Now Billy came up and smashed a long fly over the left fielder's head, and Dot and I stood up howling, "Run, run, run!" Billy rounded the bases and two runs were in.

Andy Robinson put a surprise bunt down the first-base line which Artie never even saw. Laurie got a nice hit and slid into second. Whereupon the Giants took out their pitcher and put in Buddy Williams, whom Laurie once beat up on the way to school.

Next thing we knew, the score was tied, and Dot and I were both yelling when Ernie Harrow came up for the second time and hit a home run. We were leading 8–6 when the inning ended.

Little League games are six innings, so we had five more to go. The play tightened up as the boys got over their stage fright, and by the middle of the fifth the Braves were leading 9–8. Then in the bottom of the fifth Artie missed a throw at first, and the Braves scored another run. Neither Dot nor I said a word, but Marian excused herself and went to sit on the other side of the field.

"Marian's gotten very touchy lately, don't you think?" I remarked.

In the top of the sixth George Harper, who had been pitching well for the Braves, began to tire and walked the first two batters. The third Giant hit a little fly which fell in short center field, and one run came in, making the score 10–9. Then Georgie walked the next batter, filling the bases.

"Oh, no," Dot said suddenly, "don't you dare, you can't *do* it." I stood up and began to wail, "No, no, no." The manager was motioning toward Laurie and Billy to come in as a new battery. Dot said, "He *can't* do it. Don't let him."

"That's my little boy," she explained to a man sitting on the other side of her.

"It's too much to ask of the children," I said.

But Laurie was warming up now, throwing slowly and carefully, with a windup he could only have learned from television. I said to Dot, "He doesn't look very nervous," but then my voice failed and I finished, "does he?" in a sort of gasp.

The batter was Jimmie Hill, who already had three hits. Laurie's first pitch hit the dust at Billy's feet, and Billy sprawled full-length to stop it and the crowd laughed. I said to Dot that I thought I would be getting on home. Laurie's second pitch sent Billy rolling again, and a man behind us said maybe the kids thought they were playing football or something, and Dot turned and said, "Sir, that catcher is my son."

"I beg your pardon, ma'am, I'm sure," the man said.

The umpire called Laurie's next pitch ball three, although it was clearly a strike, and I was yelling, "You're blind, you're blind!" The man behind us said that *this* pitcher wasn't going to last long, and I clenched my fist and turned around and said, "Sir, that pitcher is *my* son. If there are any more personal remarks . . ."

"Strike," the umpire said.

The man behind us announced with some humility that he hoped *both* teams would win, and subsided into silence.

Laurie then pitched two more strikes, his nice fast ball. At this point Dot and I moved down next to the fence. "Come on, Billy boy," Dot was saying, and I was telling Laurie, "Only two more outs and we win, only two more outs . . ."

"He can't hit it, Laurie," Dot yelled, "this guy can't hit," which of course was not true. The batter was Bob Weaver, and he was standing there swinging his bat and sneering.

"Strike," the umpire said, and I leaned my forehead against the cool wire and said in a weak voice, "Just two more strikes. Just get two more strikes."

Laurie looked at Billy and grinned, and I could see that behind the mask Billy was grinning too. Laurie pitched, and Bob Weaver swung wildly. "Strike two," the umpire said. Dot and I held hands. Then Laurie threw the fast ball for strike three.

One out to go, and Laurie and Billy and the shortstop stood together on the mound for a minute. I hung onto the wire and promised myself that if Laurie struck out this batter I would never, never say another word to him about the mess in his room, I would not make him paint the lawn chairs, I would not . . .

"Ball one," the umpire said, and I found that I had my voice back. "Crook!" I yelled. "Blind crook!"

Laurie pitched, the batter swung and connected in a high foul back of the plate. Billy threw off his mask and tottered, staring up. The batter, the boys on the field, the umpire waited—and Dot spoke into the silence.

"William," she said, *"you catch that ball."*

Then everyone was shouting wildly, and Laurie and Billy were slapping and hugging each other. The Giants gathered around their manager and gave a cheer for the Braves, and the Braves gathered around *their* manager and gave a cheer for the Giants, and then Laurie and Billy came pacing together toward the dugout, past Dot and me.

I said, "Laurie?" and Dot said, "Billy?" and they stared at us without recognition for a minute. Then they smiled and Billy said, "Hi, Ma," and Laurie said, "You see the game?"

PHRASE MAKERS

A HOUSE PAINTER has this advice stenciled on his truck: "Love Thy Neighbor, Paint Thy House."

—Contributed by Ralph Postiglione

CALIFORNIA GAS-COMPANY AD offering free estimate on insulation: "People without insulation in their attic have something missing upstairs."

WARNING on Connecticut highways: "He Who Has One for the Road Gets Trooper for Chaser."

BUMPER STICKER distributed by the Chamber of Commerce in Salem, Mass.: "Salem, the Witch City. Stop by for a spell."

Life in These United States® V

WE HAVE always had two cars in the family. Mine was the station wagon, big, hard to park, and difficult to find among other station wagons in parking lots. My husband's car was a pickup, four-wheel drive, forest-green, and beat-up from many hunting and fishing trips.

After years of silent suffering, I rebelled. "Why, just because we live in the country," I argued, "must we always drive a station wagon?" And I won! Our new car is a *car*—a red convertible with bucket seats and a stick shift.

Now I can always spot my car in the parking lot. My friends know when I go by. They see me and hear me. For now I'm driving the forest-green pickup with four-wheel drive.

—Jacqueline Cundiff *(Red Bluff, Calif.)*

LEAVING our apartment building one morning, my husband and I noticed water running off the outside balcony of an apartment on the second floor. Visualizing an overflowing bathtub or ruptured hot-water tank, we rushed to notify the manager. "It's okay," he said with a laugh. "The young man in 203 has been transferred to San Francisco, and he's draining his waterbed."

—Mrs. J. W. Irvine *(Seatle, Wash.)*

A COLLEAGUE of mine was asked to account for his influence with local politicians. "It's easy," he explained. "I put the bumper stickers on *after* the election."

—Thomas D. Jones, Jr. *(Hanover, Va.)*

I WAS LISTENING to my Citizens Band radio when I heard a sexy female voice say, "Breaker One Nine for Robin Hood. Are you out there, Robin Hood?" A long silence followed, and she asked the question again, but there was no answer. She tried a third time for Robin Hood, and this time a male voice answered, "Lady, would you settle for one of his Merry Men?"

—A. Brooks Harlow, Jr. *(Southborough, Mass.)*

AFTER buying our new home, we landscaped it. Since this was my husband's first attempt to plant a lawn, he was careful to do the job right. He prepared the soil, put in a sprinkler system and waited. Finally, after work, on a day when the weather was exactly right, he seeded the lawn, rolled it and watered it—finishing by artificial light because it got so late.

For the next three weeks he watered the lawn daily, often rushing home at noon to run the sprinklers for an hour. He fussed over it, shooed away birds and our cat, and looked for the first blade of grass to peek through. Except for a few weeds, nothing happened. Then one Saturday morning my husband came in and announced sheepishly, "I just found the sack of grass seed—in the garage."

"What in the world did you plant?" I asked.

With a sigh, he replied, "Kitty Litter."

—Ruth N. Kohl *(Redding, Calif.)*

WE HAD quite a large wedding, and throughout the preparations I was understandably nervous. My fiancé, however, was the picture of nonchalance, allowing neither major problems nor minor details to ruffle him. He maintained his calm even during the ceremony. As I met him at the altar, he smiled happily and asked, "New dress?"

—Carmen P. Santos *(Alexandria, Va.)*

WHEN I was a personnel manager, one of my favorite techniques in interviewing prospective salesmen was to hand them my cigarette lighter and say, "Try to sell me this lighter."

One day, after listening to applicants stumbling through various pitches, I was surprised and amused by a bright young applicant. He picked up my ligher, looked at it, put it in his pocket, sat back and said, "For ten dollars you can have your lighter back."

—L. N. Bradford *(Hopkins, Minn.)*

MY SISTER and her teen-age daughter were watching a 1930s film on TV. As it ended with the usual romantic clinch and fadeout of that era, my niece observed, "Gosh, Mom, your movies ended where ours begin."

—Mrs. H. M. Byrd *(Fresno, Calif.)*

ARRIVING in southern California from Connecticut, we acquired the services of a real-estate agent to help us find a home. He was a native Californian, and as he drove us about he praised the wonders of his state. We were used to eastern greenery and were dismayed at the dried condition of the mountainsides and the lawns of parched brown grass. When I commented on this, our agent replied in astonishment, "But my dear, this is the *golden* season!"

—M. S. Belcher *(San Diego, Calif.)*

ARRIVING in Memphis after many years' absence, I was pleasantly surprised by the architecture of the airport terminal. I asked my cabdriver when it was built, and about the other buildings under construction. Obviously an old-timer, he answered my questions and then concluded his recital of facts with: "And they ain't done yet. They're gonna improve it even worse!"

—Sheldon R. Rappaport *(Newton Square, Pa.)*

ON A VISIT to my neighbor's house, I found her busy at her ironing board. Beside her on a long rack was an orderly row of wash-and-wear shirts. As I watched, she took one shirt from its hanger, made a swipe at the collar with her hot iron, and hung it back in its place.

She continued in this manner until the bewildered look on my face forced her to explain: "Oh, I always do this. I'm pressing down the little tags that say, 'Never Needs Ironing.'"

—Mrs. Curtis Marx *(Madison, Wis.)*

AT THE golden-agers' weekly meeting, conversation turned to aches and pains. One described her arthritic joints, another gave the latest report on the hardening of his arteries, one old gentleman detailed his stomach distress—all with considerable general comment. "Well, it just proves one thing, Hilda," one woman finally said to her neighbor. "Old age sure ain't for sissies."

—Ruth S. Hain *(Castro Valley, Calif.)*

Limericks Are
Jovial Things

By WILLIAM S. BARING-GOULD

After being a judge in a limerick contest, actor-director Mike Nichols said, "It was easy. We just threw out the dirty limericks and gave the prize to the one that was left." Bearing that in mind, here are a few of the best of all time:

> *There once was a sculptor named Phidias*
> *Whose manners in art were invidious:*
> > *He carved Aphrodite*
> > *Without any nightie,*
> *Which startled the ultrafastidious*

> *According to experts, the oyster,*
> *In its shell—or crustacean cloister—*
> > *May frequently be*
> > *Either he or a she*
> *Or both, if it should be its choice-ter.*
> > > —Berton Braley

President Woodrow Wilson has been credited with this gem:

> *I sat next to the duchess at tea;*
> *It was just as I feared it would be:*
> > *Her rumblings abdominal*
> > *Were truly phenomenal,*
> *And everyone thought it was me!*

There was a young man of Laconia,
Whose mother-in-law had pneumonia.
  He hoped for the worst—
  And after March first
They buried her 'neath a begonia.

A young girl who was no good at tennis
But at swimming was really a menace,
  Took pains to explain,
  "It depends how you train;
I was a streetwalker in Venice."

There was a young girl of old Natchez
  Whose garments were always in patchez.
    When comment arose
    On the state of her clothes,
    She drawled, "When Ah itchez,
      Ah scratchez."
                              —Ogden Nash

A thrifty young fellow of Shoreham
Made brown paper trousers and woreham;
  He looked nice and neat
  Till he bent in the street
To pick up a pin; then he toreham.

There was a young lady named Bright
Whose speed was far faster than light;
  She went out one day,
  In a relative way,
And returned on the previous night.
                         —A. H. Reginald Buller

Put Your
Best Foot Backward

●II●II●II●II●II●II●II●II●II●II●II●II●II●II●II●II●II●II●II●II●II●

By WILL STANTON

●II●II●II●II●II●II●II●II●II●II●II●II●II●II●II●II●II●II●II●II●II●

THERE'S an old folk expression that says you can't have too
much of a good thing. To this I would like to add another old
expression: The heck you say.

When I was a kid I thought you could never get enough
chicken. A big hen stewed with dumplings and golden gravy
was the food of the gods. So when I saw the ad for stewing
hens at a dollar each, I called up and ordered a dozen.

Maggie wanted to know what we could do with so many.
"Stew them," I said. "Put the meat and stock in jars and freeze
it. Then some cold winter's night we want chicken and dumplings, there it is."

The man at the farm had said he'd bring them in the next
day. When I got home I found the garage doors closed and two
dogs and a cat sniffing at the cracks.

"What the devil is going on?" I asked Maggie.

She pointed to the garage. "Some cold winter's night we
want chicken and dumplings, there it is."

It turned out the man had delivered them alive, and they
were all over the garage. Apparently they had tried to roost on
the shelf where I kept my paint and it fell down. Feathers and
paint everywhere you looked. I put on old clothes and managed
to get the hens in the trunk of the car. Maggie was very little
help. Her contribution was taking pictures and singing "The
12 Days of Christmas."

After I got back, I threw my clothes in the basement and
got in the tub. Maggie came in. "What did you do with the
chickens?" she asked.

"Gave them to a poor family out in the country."

"Oh? What did they say?"

"I don't know," I told her. "They weren't home."

A few days later I took my car down to Mac's to have the tires rotated. Mac opened the trunk to get the spare. He looked down at all the red and blue chicken tracks and the white and yellow ones. He didn't say anything.

I cleared my throat. "I was taking some chickens out to the country and the paint wasn't dry."

He bounced the spare down on the concrete. "That's what I figured," he said.

I ALWAYS mean well. Everybody says that. People I barely know say it. And I like to surprise people, which is the reason I sent away for the ladybug beetles. Maggie had always had trouble with bugs on her roses and geraniums; the ladybugs were just what she needed to get rid of them. She wasn't home when they arrived—4500 of them in a plastic container. I was going to take them right out to the garden, but then I decided to wait and let Maggie see them.

I was in the living room reading the paper when I felt something on my wrist. It was a ladybug. There was another on my paper—three of them in fact. They were coming down the hall in waves. I ran out to the kitchen and found the cat had knocked the container off the table. It was empty. I could hear Maggie coming in the drive.

There has to be a stronger word than flabbergasted because that's what Maggie was. She looked at the printing on the container. "If any bean thrips or alfalfa weevils come in this house," she said, "God help them."

That evening our friends Al and Sylvia dropped in. Al brushed a beetle off his forehead and another off his sleeve. "You sure have a lot of ladybugs around here," he said.

Maggie fished one out of her drink. "Forty-five hundred," she said.

Sylvia looked at her in surprise. "You actually counted them?"

"Not exactly," Maggie said. "What you do is count the legs and divide by six." And she started to laugh. It must have been ten minutes before we got her quieted down.

I HAD read a piece about how to make a toy house out of bottle caps, but it required several hundred. So I told Roy and Sammy

I'd take all they could find at five for a cent. I wanted them to find out what it was like to earn money instead of having everything handed to them.

Hours later they came in carrying a shopping bag brimful of caps. And they had three more bags outside. Most of the caps were from beer or ale bottles. They had run into a onetime friend of mine named Ernie B. Cahoon, who said he thought it was wonderful for two boys to be doing that for their dad and he wanted to help. So he drove them to every saloon in town.

"Wasn't that nice of him?" Roy asked.

"Lovely."

"He said it was his pleasure," Sammy said.

"I'm sure of that," I said.

I kept the bags in the hall closet for a few weeks and then took them out to the car. Several days later Maggie said, "You know the bottle caps in the back of the car? The floor mat was wet and the bottoms came out of all the bags."

I got a shovel and drove to the dump. After a few minutes I noticed that the fellow unloading the next car kept looking at me out of the corner of his eye. I straightened up. "In case you're wondering," I said, "these aren't all from my family."

"Yeah," he said. "But I thought the city picked up the trash from the taverns."

"I wouldn't know," I said. "I don't work in a tavern; I work in an office."

"Well," he said, "if there's ever a job open, I wish you'd let me know."

Captains Courageous

THELWELL IN *PUNCH*

"Didn't you hear me say, 'Cut the motor'?"
AL JOHNS IN *THE SATURDAY EVENING POST*

"We thought we'd had it when a gale struck us on the turnpike."
THELWELL IN *PUNCH*

"Who's Betty?"
BO BROWN IN *THE WALL STREET JOURNAL*

"Something under $500? Step this way please."
MERIDITH, GATES FEATURES

"I'm not going to be rescued by Bob and Vera Harrington."
THELWELL IN *PUNCH*

Laughingstock
of Oat Hill

●ⅡO●ⅡO●ⅡO●ⅡO●ⅡO●ⅡO●ⅡO●ⅡO●ⅡO●ⅡO●ⅡO●ⅡO●ⅡO●ⅡO●ⅡO●

By H. B. FOX

●ⅡO●ⅡO●ⅡO●ⅡO●ⅡO●ⅡO●ⅡO●ⅡO●ⅡO●ⅡO●ⅡO●ⅡO●ⅡO●ⅡO●ⅡO●

I READ THE LETTER, smiled just a fraction, and dropped it in
the wastebasket. Only after I had begun resting my mind on
the editorial page of the Dallas *News* did the idea hit me. It
was one of those times you bust out laughing at an idea that
leaps into your brain ready-formed and raring to be done.

The letter was from my Congressman, the Hon. Nat Caxton,
Washington, D.C., and the reason I'd got it was on account
of me tearing my pants two weeks before. I'd better explain.

I had walked back to the press room, where Clyde was
printing that week's *Gazette*. Standing on tiptoe near the fly-
wheel to yell to him above the clatter of the press, I leaned
over and my pants leg caught in a belt. I got a bad cut on the
knee. Wasn't serious, but like any columnist who keeps writing
when he's got nothing to say, I wrote a little piece for my
personal column on the "hazards" of editing.

By the middle of the following week I had this letter from
Congressman Caxton on official stationery, sympathizing with
me and congratulating me on not getting hurt seriously. "I think
you're putting out a fine little paper; I never miss an issue,"
Nat wrote. He also threw in a good word for my wife, whom
he called the "little woman."

Why should a U.S. Congressman be writing a letter of
condolence for a cut knee to the editor of a country weekly?
You'll see.

Nat Caxton, or, as it was sometimes spelled in free democratic spirit, *Gnat* Caxton, had got to a seat in the councils

of the world's most powerful government the same way Warren Harding once became the head of it. Sheer luck, combined with the occasional waywardness of the democratic process.

Nat got his start in politics by preferring handshaking to hand hoeing. His first elective office after leaving the farm was justice of the peace in Castorville, two counties over from Oat Hill. To win, Nat merely shook hands with everybody—a strategy that's hard to beat.

The FBI is said, by the FBI, rarely to turn over to the courts a man who isn't guilty. The constable in Judge Caxton's precinct was better than that. Under the fee system then in use, a justice of the peace's salary was a percentage of the fines he levied. No conviction, no fine; no fine, no fee. The record in Nat's court: 100 percent convictions. You might jump to the conclusion that this strained Nat's relationship with his friends, but it didn't. His friends were never charged.

Eventually, however—probably because of an upsurge of church revivals—crime slowed in his area and Nat's salary nosedived. When it sank to $40 a month, Nat knew he had a problem. It was run for something else or go to work. Nat ran—for a seat in the Texas legislature. Since nobody else in his district wanted the job, he won hands down.

In Nat's fourth year in the legislature, the state was redistricted and Nat, seizing the opportunity, gerrymandered a new U.S. Congressional bailiwick that snaked around through this part of the state, taking in all his kinfolk and hangers-on. The following year he ran for Congress and got elected.

In Washington, Congressman Caxton wasn't very interested in international affairs, the national budget, the economic index, or the chairmanship of the Appropriations Committee. Washington was a hundred times further than he had ever calculated on getting and he settled down to staying there. The salary suited him fine, the hours were good, spittoons were furnished, the bean soup in the House restaurant was delicious, and subsidized haircuts were no more than a public servant deserved. This was a good country, he had a top-notch job, and he aimed to keep it.

But Nat made one mistake. He was too thorough. While he sent his constituents all the free seeds he could get hold of and held the record four years straight for sending out the most copies of the Agricultural Yearbook—each one personally autographed by him, meaning his secretary—he wasn't content with the ordinary. He figured out a system he estimated would keep him in Congress from then on.

Nat subscribed to every weekly newspaper in his district, all 28 of them, my own Oat Hill *Gazette* included. Then he assigned one secretary to do nothing but read all those papers, glean all the names she could, and give him a typed summary of why the names appeared.

If somebody in the district got married, Congressman Caxton immediately sent the couple a letter of congratulations and a complimentary pass to the House of Representatives. When you take into account that most weddings in a rural district are not heralded as social highlights by the big dailies, you can see that getting a personal letter from their Congressman in far-off Washington left a mighty warm feeling in the hearts of the bridal couples. It gave them something to talk about along about the time they'd discovered there wasn't much to talk about, say the second or third day of marriage.

Whatever happened to a man—good luck or bad, a broken leg, a new water well, a prize at the fair, a death in the family, the first bale of cotton or twin calves—if his name got into the paper, he got a warm personal letter from Nat. Nobody gets mad at a personal letter bragging on him if he's achieved something or feeling sorry for him if he's lost something. "Well, I'll be darned, that was nice of Nat," the voter would say.

In an average year, Congressman Caxton figured, he was writing 5000 letters to his constituents, and he believed the system was building up a backlog of affection that would keep him in office permanently.

You see now why I got the letter about my cut knee and torn pants.

That week, when the press run for the *Gazette* was completed, Clyde stopped the press, lifted off the front-page form and set it on a table nearby. I unlocked the form and started taking out type while Clyde, still wondering if I knew what I was doing, brought over a couple of trays of new type, complete with headlines. We put this new type in, locked up the page, put it back on the press and ran off half a dozen copies.

I took five of them up to my office and put them in my safe. The other one was carefully wrapped and addressed to the Hon. Nat Caxton, M.C., House Office Building, Washington, D.C., and, after making sure the regular copy that would have gone to him didn't, I dropped the special one in the mail sack along with the other papers.

What I had done was sort of tamper with the news a little in that special copy going to the Congressman. About half the leading citizens of Oat Hill were reported as having been in some mishap or were in "the news" for one reason or another:

Arthur and Agnes Struthers, who had been married 35 years but had no children, were reported to have a new son, named Nat Caxton Struthers. Banker Jonathon Carp, having stepped off the curb while reaching for a quarter he'd spotted, had fallen and broken his leg. A disastrous fire had swept the south side of the courthouse square. The other three sides of the square were saved only by the heroic efforts of the Oat Hill Volunteer Fire Department. Fire Chief Sam Brady, overcome by heat and smoke while manning a fire hose, was recovering. John Honeycut, Oat Hill's 68-year-old bachelor, was reported married to a young widow from Houston. Jimmie Hines, who had dropped out of high school two years before because he found racking balls at Dick's Pool Hall more fascinating, was reported valedictorian of his class.

Well, you can imagine the shock and confusion when, along about the middle of the next week, letters started arriving in Oat Hill from Congressman Caxton.

"Dear Jonathon," the letter to banker Carp began. "Awfully sorry to learn of your painful accident, but hope the bone is now mending satisfactorily and you can be back in your office before too long. The country needs sound, conservative banking like you're furnishing the good people of Altha County."

"What accident is he talking about?" banker Carp sputtered. "Mending bones? What's gone wrong with that lightweight we got in Washington?"

"Fire?" Chief Brady wanted to know. "We haven't had a fire in three months."

"Married!" bachelor Honeycut bellowed. "Why, they better take Nat out and have his head examined."

"I wouldn't name a pet coon after him," Arthur Struthers declared.

And what was said around at the pool hall about the letter congratulating Jimmie Hines on his fine scholastic record is not news that's fit to print.

In all, about 35 people around Oat Hill were either hopping mad or splitting their sides laughing over those crazy, haywire letters from Congressman Caxton. And the following week, when I carried a big story in the *Gazette* about it and took my copies of the doctored edition out of the safe and showed them around town, the word spread, and Congressman Caxton became the laughingstock of our district.

Needless to say, it destroyed the Congressman's confidence in the press. Not knowing when some other paper was going to doublecross him, he was left with nothing much to do in Washington but eat bean soup.

Well, it beat him. A politician can survive nearly anything except being hooted at. If he'd stuck to seeds and Agricultural Yearbooks he might have been there yet. Lots of others no better qualified are.

Last I heard of Nat, he was running for justice of the peace once more over in Castorville; said his Washington background and familiarity with sessions of the Supreme Court, which he had visited on several occasions, equipped him for real service in the justice-of-the-peace court.

I hope he gets elected.

The Art Buchwald Crash-Diet Plan

By ART BUCHWALD

LAST SUMMER I decided to go on a crash diet guaranteed to make me lose 20 pounds in a month. It consisted of coffee or tea in the morning and nothing else. For lunch: grilled meat, no salt; seven ounces of green vegetable, no salt; two ounces of Gruyère cheese or one ounce of yogurt; choice of an orange or an apple. The same went for dinner. I was allowed only a pint of water a day.

The first day was fine. Although I fainted twice, I managed to get through the day by going to bed at eight.

The next morning my wife insisted an egg with breakfast wouldn't hurt me, and since she is wiser than I am in these matters (she weighs only 119), I assumed she knew what she was talking about.

At noon I lunched with a friend who told me I was only kidding myself. "Meat is more fattening than potatoes," he said. "My doctor lets me eat all the potatoes I want—without butter, of course." I have always respected this friend's judgment (he's made a million dollars in the stock market), so I had potatoes with my meat.

In the evening I dined at the home of a wine dealer. He was shocked to think I wouldn't drink with my dinner. He pointed out that wine is a great digestive aid and unless I digested my food correctly it would automatically turn to fat. It made sense, and I had a half bottle of a very extraordinary and honest Burgundy.

The next day things went a little better. A pal said that one teaspoon of cream is about three times as fattening as one teaspoon of sugar, so I had sugar in my coffee instead of cream.

Another friend said doing without salt at meals is foolish because this only reduces the water in the body, which isn't fat, and it would come back as soon as I went off the crash diet.

A third friend told me that the best way to lose weight is to eat nothing but starches. His brother-in-law lost ten pounds that way. I've always been fond of spaghetti, and I had a bowl for lunch just to see if his brother-in-law knew what he was talking about.

In the evening my wife reported that her hairdresser said fresh lobster or shrimp or crabmeat were non-fattening, and since she couldn't remember which one I liked, she bought all three. I couldn't remember either, so I ate all of them.

The fourth day is always the hardest when you're on a crash diet, I was told. If you can get by it, the rest of the month is easy. I got by it by having scrambled eggs and toast for breakfast, chicken à la king for lunch and a cheese soufflé for dinner. It wasn't such a hard day; it's all in the mind.

I'm still continuing the crash program, but I've lined up a new set of people to eat with. Each has his own ideas about dieting, and I'm willing to listen to everybody. The main thing is not to go it alone. You need friends. If it weren't for the people who've encouraged me already, I don't think I would ever make it.

P.S.

NEAR the busy terminal of a trucking firm in Paterson, N.J., a large billboard proclaimed: "This Is a Trucking Company That Never Sleeps." Crayoned neatly beneath was: "And neither do its neighbors!"

—Contributed by James F. McNaboe

All in a Day's Work III

AFTER *Time* magazine put out a special Bicentennial issue, the editor received this letter from Harry Liversiedge of Memphis: "As a postal employe, I have naturally been concerned with delays in mail service. But imagine my horror when I recently delivered your issue dated July 4, 1776!"

WHEN a Vancouver librarian retired, her colleagues presented her with a beautiful silver bracelet bearing this inscription: "Shhhhhhhhh."

—Contributed by W. W. Bride

AS A rookie in the Atlantic City, N.J., police department, I was assigned a beat on the boardwalk. Hardly a day went by when I didn't come upon a child who had become separated from his parents.

One afternoon, I spotted a small boy standing alone, obviously lost. I tried first to gain his confidence—I took him to the nearest ice-cream stand and bought him a cone. Time passed with no sign of the boy's parents, so the next step was to call for a patrol car to take him to headquarters. I told the small fry to stay put while I went to the call box. When I returned, he was nowhere in sight.

Within minutes, the car arrived, and one of the patrolmen asked me where the child was. I felt stupid; it's humiliating to say you've lost a lost child. But I told the officers what had happened and gave a description of the boy. "What did you treat him to?" asked one of the men.

"An ice-cream cone. Why?"

"Because," answered the officer, "that kid lives only a few blocks from here, and you're about the fifth rookie he's conned for a treat!"

—Contributed by Carlton J. Duncan

MY FRIEND John and I, determined to see the world, signed on a Norwegian freighter as deckhands. We were being trained as helmsmen, and John's first lesson was given by the mate, a seasoned but gentle white-haired seafarer. John was holding the heading he had been given, when the mate ordered, "Come starboard."

Pleased at knowing immediately which way starboard was, John left the helm and walked over to his instructor. The mate had an incredulous look on his face as the helm swung freely, but he merely asked politely, "Could you bring the ship with you?"

—Contributed by Bruce Ingraham

I USED TO SELL encyclopedias door to door, and the Boston company for which I worked decided it could do well selling in northern Vermont. Few of our competition's salespeople, it was reasoned, would have traveled that far north.

On the drive up, I greedily thought about all the money I would make. Eagerly I knocked on my first door. "Hi, I'm Gene Callahan. I just came all the way up here from Boston to see you."

The Vermonter looked me up and down. "Oh. And what couldn't you sell in Boston, Gene?"

—Contributed by Eugene H. Callahan, Jr.

OUR COMPANY, along with numerous others in the United States, is involved in a program to convert from traditional English units of measurement to the metric system. All employes are encouraged to "Think Metric." The manager of our department, B. W. Miles, arrived at the office one morning to find that the nameplate on his door had been changed to: "B. W. 1.6 kms."

—Contributed by Frederick D. McFee

"Important:
Read This Carefully"

By COREY FORD

EVERYTHING comes with directions these days. No household appliance is complete without a ten-page booklet explaining how to put it together, where to install it, which way to wind it, when to change the filters and what to do if it starts humming. It's hard enough to cope with the gadgets themselves, let alone trying to understand the explanations.

You can't do anything any more without being told how. There are shaving instructions with your electric razor, refill instructions with your ballpoint pen, dry-cleaning instructions with your shirt, and zipper instructions with your pants. A bottle of aspirin contains more literature nowadays then pills. I know that the manufacturers are trying to make my life simple, but I'm getting more confused all the time.

Even familiar products arrive with an elaborate set of directions now. The other day I bought a tube of toothpaste, and it said on the box: "To remove cap, turn counterclockwise by gripping knurl. Important: do *not* tilt." Now, I've been taking the tops off toothpaste tubes all my life, but the more I studied this description the harder the operation seemed. I got a good firm grip on the knurl and turned counterclockwise until I began tilting. Finally the bottom of the tube split open and the contents squirted down my sleeve. Fortunately there's still a little paste left in the old tube, and its cap has been missing for months.

My house is cluttered with guidebooks and charts I can't throw away. I have a drawerful of instructions for things I'm supposed to do once a year, like draining the oil in the freezing unit or winding my 400-day clock. "This lighter is guaranteed for 18 months," a folder states. "To replace flint..." Not only do I have to remember what the directions say; 18 months later I have to remember where I put them.

The trouble is that I can't absorb directions. Let me pick up a folder that starts, "For best results read this carefully," or "Congratulations! You are now the proud owner of a Little Demon Home Distillery. The enclosed manual will help you to..." and right away my mind goes wandering off. I'm mentally shading all the O's and Q's in the diagrams and drawing imaginary mustaches on the figures in the illustrations. Maybe it's because the authors of those manuals can make a simple task like threading a needle sound as involved as operating a computer.

Take garden seeds, for example. I can remember when all you had to do was stick them in the ground. Not any more. Today the packet reads: "Plant to depth of 1½ times seed in well-drained friable soil between May and June (northern half U.S.) and thin to 4″ after ten days." Prescriptions on medicine bottles are just as obscure (how can you take *one* pill three times daily?), and first-aid instructions have me completely baffled. By the time I figure out how to peel open an adhesive bandage, I've almost bled to death.

Or take the case of a friend of mine who purchased a cuckoo clock in Germany. "Take first out the two wirecramps which hold together the bellows," the translation said, "and hang onto the pendulumwire the pendulum with the weights from the chains to tick straightly." He worked that out, and then he read: "The call of the cuckoo can be fetched, without that the clock strikes wrong, by pulling at the ring which hangs at the left in a string." I understand he solved the whole problem by glancing at his watch and cuckooing every hour on the hour.

What makes it all the harder is that most directions are so complicated you can remember only one sentence at a time. This means you have to keep running back to the instruction manual. Not long ago I had to put up a new antenna for the television set, and I carefully memorized the first step of the instructions: "Set upright pole (Y) into base receptacle (W²) so that grooves in slot match screw holes (Fig. 7)." Repeating this to myself, I climbed the ladder and set up the pole (Y), and then realized that the guidebook was lying on the back porch. So I carried the pole back down the ladder and read the second part: "Affix thumb nut (J) to bolts (JJ) and hook guy wires to terminal eyes (see preceding page)." Mumbling this incantation over and over so I wouldn't forget it, I carried the pole up the ladder again—by which time Part One had completely slipped my mind. I ended up by sticking the antenna in the lawn—which may explain why we've been getting such poor reception lately.

Women don't seem to have the same trouble with directions as men, but this is because they make up their own as they go along. My wife has a prize collection of recipes, but whenever she sets out to cook something, she simply adds a pinch of this and a dash of that. When it comes to giving directions to somebody else, though, a woman is a veritable model of efficiency.

Last weekend we invited some people for supper, and while my wife was busy in the kitchen I started to tidy up the living room. I got the vacuum cleaner hitched up all right, but when I pressed the starter button nothing happened. Whereupon the following dialogue ensued:

Me *(shouting to kitchen):* Darling, how do you get this vacuum to start?

Wife *(shouting back):* Just push that little thing in front.

Me *(after a vain search):* What little thing, dear?

Wife *(over rattle of pots and pans):* It's that sort of a funny-looking gadget on top of the whatchamacallem.

Me: Which whatchamacallem?

Wife *(spelling it out):* Look under the whosis. You'll see a thingumajig right next to the big flat doohickey, and beside it is a small round gimmick. Well, it's the little doodad in back of the other one. *(Sound of oven door slamming.)* Never mind, I'll vacuum the living room myself. Honestly, you men are all alike.

ON THE other hand, *I* can give directions very clearly. If you're planning to drive to our house, for instance, just stop at the filling station and ask the attendant how to get here. He's the one who always tells me.

TRUTH OR ERROR?

My MOTHER was telling us of a new cookbook by a Scottish priest. "It's a book of Highland recipes," she said, "with a little antidote beside each one."

—Contributed by G. H. Macdonald

HELP-WANTED ad in the Syracuse *Herald-Journal:* "Janitor to work nights, 5-day week. Moping, cleaning, etc."

AD IN the program of the Snowden Township, Pa., High School band: "A. and D. Furniture Co. Colonial and Temporary."

FROM the Philadelphia *Inquirer:* "Cars were lined up bumper-to-bumped on the three eastbound lanes."

FROM the Waukegan, Ill., *News-Sun:* "Her attorney immediately sought a five-minute recess to clam her. The trial never resumed."

FROM the personals column in the Westlake, Ohio, *West Life:* "Josephine—please take me back. It was just a passing fanny. Your George."

ON ORDER coupon: "Send no money now. You will be bilked later."

—Contributed by Ira M. Freeman

FROM an ad in the Clarksburg, W. Va., *Telegram:* "For Sale—two-bedroom cabin with naughty pine walls."

Fowl Play

"He said his first words: 'E pluribus unum.'"
J. MONAHAN IN *SATURDAY REVIEW*

"George simply loves playing with the children."
RODNEY JONES, INTERPRESS

"And, further, it says,
'For small birds they are remarkably strong!'"

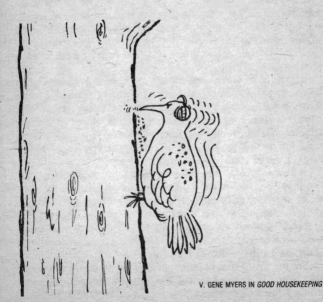

So You Want the Right Tool for the Job?

By DERECK WILLIAMSON

THE OTHER day my wife asked me to unstick the kitchen drawer again. As I hunted around for some tool to pry it open with, it occurred to me that I've been using the *wrong* tools all my life. In fact, I thought proudly, I'm probably an expert.

They say it's important to use the right tool for the right job, but actually it's not. The wrong tool can be used for the right job, and it's often handier. A silver grapefruit spoon makes a good wrong screwdriver, for example (you can usually bend it back into shape afterward). For heavier jobs, I use a shoehorn.

The right tools required most often around my house are a hammer, a screwdriver and a pair of slip-joint pliers. I own all three, but they are kept in the stuck kitchen drawer along with spatulas, corn tongs, can openers, plastic spoons, whisks, strainers, jar lids, bottle stoppers, sardine-can keys, jar openers, steak knives, corkscrews, electric-mixer beaters, fuses, napkin rings, a garlic press, snarled string and a ping-pong ball.

A screwdriver is the thing needed to stick in the drawer crack to lever down the whisk which is pushing up the corn tongs which are gripping the spatula which is holding the drawer shut. *But* the screwdriver is in the stuck drawer. (Simply trying to force the drawer not only jams it worse, but bends an electric-mixer beater. Later, in the mixer, it will make a terrible noise and fling frosting all over the walls.)

So, the wrong tool I use for opening the drawer is a captured World War I German bayonet that my uncle gave me. I located it in the linen closet behind my shoeshine kit, and in less than

15 minutes I was able to open the drawer the first time. It's a fine tool, and I'd suggest that you get one immediately. Look in your attic. Maybe your neighbor has one. Or you might get in touch with your nearest extremist group.

Even after the kitchen drawer is unstuck, however, the right tools aren't always handy. To find them you must paw through the drawer, playing a dangerous game called Kitchen Roulette. The object is to lay hands on a tool before the serrated edge of a steak knife slashes your finger off.

Rather than take that risk, I use a small wood chisel for tightening things like screws on doorknobs and cabinet hinges. If somebody actually uses the chisel for woodworking, though, it's not such a hot idea to mention that you've been using it as a screwdriver. Quietly put it back exactly where you found it. (The same rule applies when you've used somebody's carpenter level to pound in garden stakes, or his micrometer as a glue clamp.)

I find that I'm better off using the right tool for the wrong purpose. When I do run across a screwdriver, I use it for stirring paint, hammering tacks and chiseling wood (after the wood chisel has been ruined driving screws). When I try to drive screws with a screwdriver, I run into trouble.

Last week, for example, I was fixing a chair and, using a screwdriver, had succeeded in getting a woodscrew almost flush with the seat when the notch stripped and I couldn't turn the screw either way. Even the corn tongs wouldn't budge it. When I tried to pull it out with a claw hammer I had been using as a sash weight, one of the claws broke. I tried to hammer it down, but the surrounding wood rapidly became, shall we say, "over-antiqued." And the screw stuck up even higher.

I rejected the idea of hacksawing off the head of the screw because I was using the hacksaw blade to keep a window from rattling. I finally borrowed a drill from a neighbor to drill out the screw. I got most of it out before the drill slipped and the bit went into the wood and broke off. To get the bit out, I needed the claw hammer, but since that was broken I used the jar opener. That bent up the jar opener, but I open jars with a screwdriver anyway. I wound up nailing the chair seat to the loose leg, using the flat side of a pair of pliers for a hammer.

A handy thing to have around the house is a vise. Used for many repair jobs, it can make *more* repair jobs if you tighten it just a shade too much. I have used my vise for flattening curtain rods I was trying to shorten, for scarring old pictures frames I was trying to re-nail, and for pulverizing pottery I was trying to glue.

When using a vise as a clamp to line up two pieces of something prior to fastening or drilling, bear in mind that you need a minimum of three hands. Each of the two pieces to be lined up requires a hand, and a third is needed to close the jaws of the vise. If you have only two hands, you must summon a small child to work the crank. He will be delighted. He will spin the crank. He will crush your fingers.

As previously noted, pliers can be used to hammer things with. But they're really better for not gripping things with. The pliers I have owned have all had jaws I could see light between. That's because they didn't close properly. It gives me a warm feeling to know that I'll never accidentally crush an insect with my pliers.

For not picking up small things, it's handy to own a pair of needle-nose pliers with jaws you can see light between. The tool is used chiefly for punching holes in pieces of paper so they'll go in ring binders. It is not to be confused with a nail punch, which makes air holes in insect-jar lids.

Slip-joint pliers have a clever mechanical arrangement which allows you to widen the jaws so that, when gripping something, the ends of the handles can snap together and pinch your palm. A quick shift of the axis and you're back to an ordinary pair of pliers with jaws you can see light between. Special wire-cutting jaws at the bottom of the "V" will gnaw through a piece of wire almost as fast as a pair of nail scissors will.

You can also cut wire with a hammer and a screwdriver. But they're in the kitchen drawer. And that—you guessed it— is stuck again.

FROM A WILMETTE, ILL., *Deerfield Review* article about an exercise class: "Slacks a but too tight?"

Humor in Uniform III

●I●|●I●|●I●|●I●|●I●|●I●|●I●|●I●|●I●|●I●|●I●|●I●|●I●|●I●|●I●|●I●

●I●|●I●|●I●|●I●|●I●|●I●|●I●|●I●|●I●|●I●|●I●|●I●|●I●|●I●|●I●|●I●

INEPT at replacing a missing button on my pajamas, I was delighted when a charming WREN (Women's Royal Naval Service) officer, billeted in the same London hotel, promised to sew one on for me. The following day, my company received urgent orders to move. I dashed down the corridor to the WREN's room, only to find that her fiancé had just arrived. "I'm terribly sorry to barge in like this," I stammered breathlessly. "I've come for my pajamas."

—B. H. Smith *(Penrith, England)*

WHILE I was driving through a Navy installation recently, I listened to the base's radio station in my car. At one station break, the announcer gave the time: "It is now eight bells." After a brief pause: "For you Air Force personnel, that is 1600 hours." After a longer pause: "And for you Marines, the big hand is on . . ."

—B. D. R. *(APO, San Francisco, Calif.)*

AN AIR FORCE pilot was flying a mission over the Mekong Delta one morning when someone on the same radio frequency started blowing into his microphone as if to test it. This disturbing noise continued every few minutes for some time. Finally, out of the blue, without any radio procedure, a thoroughly Australian accent came on the air: "Mate, ya bin blowin' in me ear for 'alf an hour now. When ya goin' ta kiss me?"

—1st Lt. Gary L. Nickerson *(APO, San Francisco, Calif.)*

POINTING to a pan of chicken wings and legs disguised in the

237

classic messhall manner, a young airman asked the mess sergeant, "What's for chow?"

"Air Force chicken," replied the sergeant. "You want wings or landing gear?"

—2nd Lt. Paul Jagger, USAF *(Colorado Springs, Colo.)*

AT A tense debriefing, after an attack on our base in Vietnam, one young airman described his actions in this measured fashion: "As the incoming rounds began exploding in the vicinity of our building, I sounded the siren alarm. I then initiated a thorough inspection of the office and, after satisfying myself that all classified documents were secured, I locked the safe and proceeded to inspect the security files to see that they were closed. After completing these precautions, I donned my combat gear and made an orderly exit down the hallway and into the bunker outside."

The commander, obviously impressed, asked, "And approximately how much time elapsed from the start of the attack until you reached your bunker, son?"

Replied our hero, "Oh, I'd say about three seconds. sir."

—Sgt. Homer P. Walton *(McClellan AFR, Calif.)*

OUR COMMANDANT in military school, a retired general, constantly harassed the cadets about wearing their dress hats too low on their foreheads, with the bills almost covering their eyes—a style we thought looked rather sharp. He wore his own hat pushed well back on his head, and we secretly made remarks about his looking like a bus driver.

During the first inspection of the year, the commandant singled out a new cadet and gave him five demerits for having his hat pulled down over his eyes. "But, sir," moaned the cadet, "don't you wear your hat too far back?"

There was an audible gasp throughout the comapny. "Well, son," the commandant said, "I'll tell you about that. It's *my* bus."

—R. Terry Ronner *(Wilmington, N.C.)*

THE LIFE of a soldier during wartime hasn't changed too much. Recently I read the diary my grandfather wrote during Gen. U.S. Grant's Vicksburg campaign. The notation for January 20, 1863, reads: "Still raining. Day gloomy. Bought a gallon of whiskey. Day still gloomy."

—Robert Deacon, Jr., *(La Mesa, Calif.)*

MY FRIEND in the airborne school was having trouble making his jumps from the plane. One day I tried to give him some helpful instruction. "When you get to the door," I said, "remember to look down at your hands and feet. See that they are properly placed before you jump."

"What!" he exclaimed. "You mean you open your eyes?"

—T. M. Dickie *(Gatesville, Texas)*

OUR FIELD hospital in North Africa was under canvas, and the only place we nursing sisters could bathe was in an open-air tub surrounded by screens. One girl was relaxing in the water when she suddenly realized that she was being watched. A group of mounted riders in the French Camel Corps were peering down at her from their lofty perches. Hurriedly dressing, she sought out the officer in charge of the unit and complained about his men's behavior.

"I can assure you, sister," the Frenchman said soothingly, "that you have no need at all for alarm. Not one of those men can speak English."

—Romola Showell *(Sutton Coldfield, England)*

WHILE SERVING in a remote area of Southeast Asia, I wrote my wife of the long evenings, the shortage of books and music, and the abundance of winsome lasses. I mused that I might fill the lonely hours learning to play a harmonica, if I had one. By return mail came a harmonica.

When I finally returned home, I was met at the airport by my wife, who said, "All right, first things first. Let's hear you play that harmonica!"

—Capt. Bruce Simnacher *(San Antonio, Texas)*

RECENTLY, I overheard a conversation between two New Yorkers. One had just reported aboard the U.S. Naval Air Facility in Sigonella, Sicily, and the other, an old-timer of three months' duty, offered him these comforting words: "If you get homesick, come on over to my locker. I've got a map of the subway."

—SK3 E. Stroman *(FPO, New York, N.Y.)*

The Case
of the Jolly Jailbirds

◉◉◉◉◉◉◉◉◉◉◉◉◉◉◉◉◉◉◉◉◉◉◉◉◉◉◉◉◉◉◉◉◉◉◉

By TONI HOWARD

◉◉◉◉◉◉◉◉◉◉◉◉◉◉◉◉◉◉◉◉◉◉◉◉◉◉◉◉◉◉◉◉◉◉◉

IT STARTED in May 1946, when Fernand Billa, a minor French prison official who looks something like a Roman senator, lumbered into the little Norman town of Pont-l'Evêque to take over as chief warden of the district prison. Hounded by an unquenchable thirst, Billa couldn't quite keep his mind on prison administration. So, Pont-l'Evêque soon got used to seeing its new warden rolling from café to café in search of one more *petit Calva*, a native double-distilled applejack.

Inside the jail, unkept prison ledgers and unopened mail piled up on Billa's desk, and 50 neglected convicts were locked away indiscriminately.

And then into this unholy disorder, eyes shining with zeal behind tortoise-shell glasses, came an angel of rescue named René Grainville. Once from the Pont-l'Evêque area himself, Grainville was a rotund, bald-headed little man with a pixie smile and a quiet, efficient manner. A former accountant, journalist, *Résistance* hero, poet and philosopher, he had been sent up for two years for a slight affair of forgery and embezzlement.

Within one hour of his arrival, Grainville had sized up Billa's gentle, thirsting nature, slipped out of his cell block, walked into Billa's office and offered two bottles of *pastis* and his services as "prison accountant." Billa was impressed. "Shh!" he said to an open-mouthed guard. "This fellow's an intellectual. I'm going to put him in charge of the office."

Grainville's conception of his usefulness to the prison was a little grander than that. "You permit me?" he said and, sitting down at Billa's desk, started studying some of the documents.

"Ah, I see." He adjusted his spectacles. "Now the first thing is for me to get your signature down pat, so you won't have to be troubled signing these things. . . ."

Grainville practiced signing while Billa watched, fascinated. *"Formidable!"* he breathed.

Grainville's smile was modest. "Now these registers," he said briskly. "You don't happen to have a decent counterfeiter in the house?"

But yes, a young hood who had once worked in the legal archives of the police department in Lyon had quite a reputation for falsifying documents. "Send him down," said Grainville; "we may need to rough out a couple of official stamps."

Then the phone rang. Grainville picked it up. "Chief Warden Billa speaking," he said, and reassured Billa with a polite whisper: "It's just the judge calling from the courthouse. I'll handle it."

That night Billa made his usual tour of the village bars with a lightened heart. Things were at last in the hands of an expert.

They were indeed. After studying the penitentiary code briefly, Grainville tossed it in the wastebasket as anti-social nonsense and instituted a code of his own. His code, as he told the judge at his trial last fall, was based on "making life a little less painful for my fellow prisoners."

First, he selected as his assistants those convicts who had what he called "background"—that is, a certain amount of money and a useful skill. With a butcher turned car thief running the cuisine, a bartender who had specialized in fencing stolen goods handling the wines and liquors, and a former hotelkeeper known as "Georges the Shark" (up for armed robbery) in charge of ordering such outside delicacies as well-heeled prisoners would buy, an organized abundance soon reigned in the quartermaster department.

All restrictions on card-playing, cigarettes and liquor were discarded. A tailor-pickpocket was detailed to take care of the prisoners' clothes. A telephone hookup with a bookmaker in the nearby gambling resort of Deauville accommodated the horse-players. Grainville then made the prison co-educational, according to later newspaper reports, by throwing open the doors between the men's and women's wings.

Almost overnight the prison of Pont-l'Evêque, under its trail-blazing new guest director, took on the characteristics of a small family hotel. Certain extras cost money, of course—

the lobster, the vintage wines, the morning newspaper delivered with breakfast—but everything else was on the house.

Yet even in the midst of such well-ordered luxury, the inmates showed a certain restlessness. With Billa staggering freely in and out, it was inevitable that others would get ideas. Thus Jean Manguy, a former Paris gangster, refused to order up his breakfast in bed but insisted instead on traipsing across the square every morning in his sumptuous blue Japanese bathrobe to take his coffee and *croissant* in the corner café. Thus, too, a bookmaker was too tame for horse-players like Nova the Fence and Georges the Shark; they themselves wanted to drive over and see the horses running at the Deauville track seven miles away. And the ones who wanted to pub-crawl all night with Billa!

It was a problem to unnerve a less philosophical man than René Grainville. But Grainville's Code had the solution: Put the men on their honor. And in defense of the system it must be said that, except for one case, it worked.

The lone defection was more a credit than demerit to Grainville's system. News of the little prison's comforts had spread, and criminals serving time elsewhere began to plot to get in. A new arrival in March 1949 was a notorious holdup man and escape artist known as René the Cane. He had confessed to a crime in Normandy which he hadn't committed, in order to get moved from a big hermetic Paris prison to something less formal. For a month René the Cane stuck it out at Pont-l'Evêque, but then the habit of a lifetime became too strong and he took it on the lam. Not by walking out the front door, however, which was wide open, but in the classic tradition: he sawed through the window bars and swung down on a rope, "so as not to cause any trouble for my friend the warden."

It was heart-warming, really, the way Billa's prisoners looked out for his welfare. Once they went out late at night to locate their wandering warden and trundle him safely home in a wheelbarrow. Several times, when the guards were otherwise engaged, the prisoners punched the time-clocks themselves so that all would look well for the Billa administration.

Strange prison, where the prisoners weren't imprisoned, the warden didn't ward and the district inspector didn't inspect too much! Actually, the district inspector did show up occasionally. One day he did criticize the cobwebs on the basement ceiling. Billa stammered something.

"He never sees them," explained Grainville. "He's too busy watching his feet."

On another occasion the inspector told Billa that he was drinking too much. "Yes, sir!" said Billa enthusiastically.

Also the inspector felt that the front door ought to be kept locked.

"Oh, you know, *M'sieu l'Inspecteur*," said Grainville, "they're good boys."

In time, of course, with convicts wandering around freely, the villagers began to take notice. One of the first was a lawyer who, presenting himself at the prison to confer with a convict client, was told by a guard, "Just a moment, I'll see if he's in." (He wasn't.) Why, then, during the nearly four years that this happy state of affairs went on, did nobody squeal?

The villagers didn't squeal because, as they explained later, it was none of their business; it was the business of "the magistrates." Besides, they felt sorry for Billa. "He was so *gentil!*" they told me. "He wouldn't hurt a fly." And as for Grainville, they were rather more proud of him than disapproving: he was a local boy making good. Moreover, many of the villagers supplied the prison with produce, fuel and luxuries. If a scandal broke, the prison might be closed down and so would its trade. It was the same with Pont-l'Evêque's lawyers: the convicts were their clients—and their fees.

Surprisingly, Grainville himself quite clearly turned no profit from the whole affair. For all the artistry with which he embellished his fellow prisoners' police records—and a good-conduct notation was as easy to get as a three-day pass—he at no time touched his own. And for all the time he whittled off the others' sentences, he served out his own term to the minute. The blissful satisfaction of having for so long hood-winked the authorities was evidently enough reward for him. His only regret seems to be that it didn't go on forever.

Why didn't it? The Ministry of Justice, understandably sensitive about the whole affair, is not too definite. But it is known that in January of 1950 Billa was fired and the prison closed down. And in 1952 Georges the Shark, drunk and talkative in a Paris bar, got to bragging about beating a prison sentence in Pont-l'Evêque. A police inspector overheard him, and an investigation finally got under way.

So poor old Billa had to be tried, in October 1955, and condemned to three years for "negligence." Then, shortly afterward, eight members of the inside gang had to be tried—for "falsification of government documents."

The latter trial was sheer vaudeville, with Grainville, of course, heading the bill. In his role as "philanthropist," as he called himself, he politely elaborated his theories of prison reform for the judge. When the judge accused him of forging Billa's signature more than 300 times, he nodded, smiled his pixie smile and explained blandly, "I have always endeavored to give satisfaction to my employers."

The jury, seven good Normans and true, roared with laughter, and at the trial's end returned a verdict of acquittal. And that night the little village of Pont-l'Evêque celebrated the victory.

DOUBLE STANDARDS

HOLIDAYING in Spain, I was introduced to a police inspector who spoke fluent English. We became good friends and when my vacation ended he came to say *adiós*. Waving to him as I drove off, I turned the wrong way on a one-way street. A shrill whistle brought me back to reality as a policeman ran toward me, arms wide apart. Before he could throw the book at me, my friend caught up with us and dismissed the policeman. Turning to me he declared, "Anyone else, one-way street. My friends—both ways!"

—Contributed by Garside Allison

MS READ-a-thon—
a simple way to start youngsters reading

Boys and girls between 6 and 14 can join the MS READ-a-thon and help find a cure for Multiple Sclerosis by reading books. And they get two rewards — the enjoyment of reading, and the great feeling that comes from helping others.

Parents and educators: For complete information call your local MS chapter. Or mail the coupon below.

Kids can help, too!